A Year of Hope

52 Weeks of Faith and Courage

by
Ann E. Bolson, D.Min.

Ann E. Bolson

PINECONE BOOK COMPANY

A YEAR OF HOPE
52 Weeks of Faith and Courage

Copyright 2018 by Ann Bolson. All rights reserved.

This book is available for purchase at Amazon.com.

ISBN 978-1-949053-02-9

Pinecone Book Company
Evergreen, Colorado

I would like to thank Rev. Dick Donovan,
whose weekly publication known as "Sermon Writer"
helped me craft my Sunday messages for many years.
I dedicate this book to him.

I also dedicate this book to my husband Steve
for his patience and encouragement of my ministry,
as well as of my writing.

"Your soul has been waiting for you to wake up to your own existence for years. But you must start the conversation."

—ELIZABETH GILBERT, *Big Magic*

Table of Contents

Preface

In the summer of 2017, I began the ponderous task of reviewing dozens of hard copy sermons and other documents that were stashed in our garage. My motivation was to save our children from this effort when we are no longer living. To my surprise, I was unable to release the sermons, and I received a strong inner message to organize and archive them. This nudging developed into an even stronger message to summarize a full year of them and place them in a book for those who could not get to worship. "Oh, no!" implored my writer friend Jean. "This book is meant for many more people than that!"

There are scriptures and wisdom writings from many sources that can continue to inspire and guide us and renew our hope. May these words do just that for you.

Chapter 1

Advent and Hope

I am pleased to begin this collection of writings drawn from some of my previous work as a pastor in the Christian tradition. This book is meant to offer solace to the many who cannot easily attend worship or who desire "spiritual food" any time of any day. It is my hope that my reliance upon storytelling instead of the scholarly exposition of the scriptures will make this book more accessible to many readers.

I will, for the most part, depend upon the RCL, or Revised Common Lectionary, which is simply an arrangement of scripture readings in a three-year cycle so that everyone gets "a taste" of many of the writings of the Bible, New Testament and Old. There are people who would love to tell you that this or that scripture lesson should solely guide your life, but it is my belief that God will guide you on that.

The first Sunday in the church year is all about HOPE. One passage that may be read says, "The people who walked in the darkness have seen a great light; those who lived in the land of deep darkness—on them the light has shined... For a child has been born to us, a son given to us; authority rests upon his shoulders; and he is named Wonderful Counselor, Mighty God, Everlasting Father, Prince of Peace." (Isaiah 9:2,6)

Over forty years ago, I was as big as a barn and awaiting the birth of our first child. Although I was quite uncomfortable, I waddled through my days with a sense of joyful anticipation. We lived in the upper story of an old home in Davenport, Iowa. The walk-in closet was designated as the nursery. In that we had no knowledge of the gender of our child, we decorated it in lovely greens and yellows. We were filled with anticipation. Advent is a season of anticipation, of awaiting birth. My wish for each of us this Advent season is that we might learn a new way of thinking which could help birth more Christ consciousness in each of us, that we might come to see and feel and know that it was not just Jesus who was "of the Parent's heart begotten," but that we, too, originated in the heart of God.

"OF THE PARENT'S HEART BEGOTTEN" (v.1)
The New Century Hymnal

Of the Parent's heart begotten
when the worlds were yet to be,
One there was with no beginning, One who is eternally—
Source and Ending of all things that have been,
and all things that are to be,
Forever and forever.

Like Isaiah, I had a vision of my own last week as I was preparing this message. I saw a wooden table with a white cloth. There were three figures approaching the table, all representatives of the children of Abraham. The Jewish figure pushed forward a large statue of Moses and spoke loudly of the promised land. The Islamic figure pushed forward a large statue of Mohammed and spoke of his right to live in Jerusalem. The Christian figure pushed forward a large statue of Jesus and said, "No one comes to the Father but by me." Suddenly the earth shook and the statues fell apart. Behind each was now a frightened child. The living figures of their faith came up alongside them: Moses, Mohammed and Jesus. They all approached the table of grace. The Arab took off his headpiece, a reminder of the persecution his people had suffered hundreds of years ago. He said, "I no longer desire to dwell in the past." The Christian looked into his brothers' eyes and said, "I could see peace instead of this." The Jew added, "Surely God dwells in every human heart."

Will this vision ever become a reality? It starts with you and me. The possibility grows every time our ego's resentments can be calmed by the still, small voice of God, every time we can say *shalom*, "peace be with you," and *namaste*, "the God in me acknowledges the God in you." Amen.

Chapter 2

Advent and Peace

In Christianity, the prophet Isaiah is most often referenced during Advent. He had some beautiful words about God's plan for humanity, and the One who would come to save the people. There was a man in my last congregation who often read scripture for me during worship. During Advent, folks would lovingly call him "Norman **Isaiah** Milford."

Some of my favorite words from Isaiah come from Chapter 2, verse 4: "He shall judge between the nations, and shall arbitrate for many peoples; they shall beat their swords into plowshares, and their spears into pruning hooks; nation shall not lift up sword against nation, neither shall they learn war any more."

Peace is a prize that many people long for. To me, peace is like a plant that must be cultivated and nurtured in our own hearts. And all the while that we tend it, we hold **hope** that it will flourish. That which sustains us in our journey is called **faith**.

When my father was dying in 2002, he loved to remember a phrase I had once shared with him. It came from one of my daily meditation books and it said, "I don't have to know the design my life will take, I only have to trust the Designer." He didn't know if his cancer treatment would be successful. He didn't know how much time he had left. But he did know that he trusted the Designer of his life, God, and that he always had. Because of this trust and faith in God, he was able to spend the final months of his life in a type of blissful recollection of his life on this planet. He engaged in a form of life review that made it easier to release his body and return to his Source.

"Come, O Long-expected Jesus"
Chalice Hymnal

Come, O long-expected Jesus, born to set your people free.
From our fears and sins release us;
Christ in whom our rest shall be.
You, our strength and consolation,
come salvation to impart;
Dear desire of many a nation, joy of many a longing heart.

Before I was a minister, I was a psychotherapist. I once had a young client whose mother dropped her off at my doorstep and said, "Would you please fix my kid?" This teen-aged girl was using and selling drugs and had joined a gang. You see, she was in a dangerous field with the drug sales. So, if she felt threatened, she could turn to her gang for protection. The gang was her safety net, she felt.

During one session, she asked me, "Why should I stop selling drugs if no one finds out about it?" I talked to her about criminal thinking, which says, "It's not a crime if no one finds out about it." She opened up to me. We shared. She told me one day that she wanted to stop selling drugs because I'd told her that she had to become a person who could look herself in the eye every day. "I think I am going to quit selling drugs because I am becoming a little criminal," she said.

She worked out a plan with her mother, whom she had intimidated terribly with her rough language and her yelling and her disregard, and they moved to a smaller town so she could get away from the gang influence. To my knowledge, she was able to set herself straight. Hope, faith, peace and resolve had prevailed.

Chapter 3

Advent and Joy

As I type this message today, I am wearing a pink fleece jacket. This is the color ascribed to "Gaudete Sunday," the Sunday of Joy, the third Sunday of Advent, wherein the pink candle of the Advent wreath is lit. The other candles are purple, save for the white Christ candle that is lit on Christmas Eve. This particular Sunday is a celebration of the joy that Mary, the mother of Jesus, expressed after hearing from an angel that she would give birth to the "Son of the Most High." The words that Mary spoke to Elizabeth are known as "The Magnificat" and are found in Luke 1:46-55. This passage is too long to quote here, but they inspired a beautiful hymn by Miriam Therese Winter:

"My Soul Gives Glory to My God" (v.1,4)
The New Century Hymnal

My soul gives glory to my God. My heart pours out its praise.
God lifted up my lowliness in many marvelous ways.
Love casts the mighty from their thrones,
promotes the insecure,
Leaves hungry spirits satisfied, the rich seem suddenly poor.

A Roman Catholic nun once told me that Mary's body had been colonized by the Church as an expression of the ideal woman: demure, meek, mild and virginal. This sort of persona does not work for most modern women.

One year, on Gaudete Sunday, I imparted a message taken from Matthew 11:2-11. In this passage, John the Baptizer sits in prison. He sent one of his followers to Jesus to ask him this question: "Are you the one who is to come, or are we to wait for another?" Jesus answered that through him, blind received their sight, lame walked, lepers were cleansed, the deaf could hear, the dead were raised and the poor had the good news brought to them.

A pastor from Wisconsin named Mark Yurs discusses questions and answers and asks a question of us: "Do you remember when you were a child in school? Do you remember being perplexed about what the teacher was talking about, or what the textbook was supposed to tell you? Were you usually the first one to raise your hand and ask the question, or were you more likely to wait for another?" He goes on to say that it is a relief when someone else asks our question. And even better, it's a relief when the one who does not understand is the smartest kid in the class. Then we don't feel so badly about not knowing.

John asks, "Are you the one who is to come, or are we to wait for another?" It's a question we all ask, in various ways. "Is Jesus the real thing?" Or, "Is this Christmas story just a fanciful tale, charming but ultimately worthless?" These types of doubts we can all entertain at times in our lives. But we fear that to ask them is to appear faithless. However, in our story today, the hand is already in the air, and it belongs to the smartest kid in the class, John the Baptizer.

Rev. Yurs reminds us that John was in prison, and that "prison can put doubt into anybody's heart. It is easy to believe in God in the bright sunlight when all is joyful and free, but let the iron doors of difficulty slam shut, and doubt is there in the darkness." Does doubt plague your life? Perhaps you could remind yourself of some of the people you have known about who were committed to the Gospel, the good news of free grace, and used that to do important things. Rev. Martin Luther King Jr. comes to my mind. He was a powerful witness. Few of us will match his gifts, but we are all called upon to help.

Chapter 4

Advent and Love

Have you ever noticed the themes on the postage stamps of the U.S. Postal Service around Christmas time? It is usually something secular, such as botanicals or candles in the window, and also something religious, so often a portrayal of Mary and the baby Jesus. Someone is missing from that picture, and it is Joseph. Today is a day to celebrate all the men throughout history who have made the decision to raise, nurture, teach, protect and provide for children who may or may not be their own.

It is important to realize that Joseph had a number of choices in this situation wherein Mary was pregnant, but not pregnant by him. Hebrew law would have directed him to break their engagement and "dismiss her quietly." Or, she might have been stoned to death as an adulteress (as happens even now in some cultures). But scripture tells us that an angel convinced him otherwise. Yet, it is very important to realize that he did not have to stay with Mary. *He didn't have to do it.* He didn't have to subject himself to the gossip mill or be in harm's way.

"ONE CANDLE IS LIT" *Chalice Hymnal*

Come surely, Lord Jesus, as dawn follows night,
Our hearts long to greet you, as roses the light.
Salvation, draw near us, our vision engage.
One candle is lit for the hope of the age.

One of the most poignant experiences I have had in terms of performing wedding ceremonies was that of a 40-something woman with four sons and her 40-something heretofore bachelor husband. The bride had first married a man she met while working for a carnival. He was neither steady nor attentive. She let him go, or he wandered off, and she raised the four boys as a single mom. Along came a man of a different fiber. He loved her and honored her and willingly took on the job of guiding those boys who were still at home. *He didn't have to do it*, but he did.

During the homily at the wedding, I told this couple about the Jewish concept of *tikkun olam*, the healing of the world. I gave thanks that the groom was willing to participate in the healing of the father-wound that the boys had suffered. I quoted psychiatrist Frank Pittman to them, who states at the end of his book *Man Enough*, "As I've lived through my life as a man, I've learned the secrets of happiness. I pass them on to my kids, and I pass them on to you: Forgive your parents, join the team, find some work and some play to do, get a partner to do it with, keep it equal, and raise children, wherever you find them."

Pittman tells us, "Becoming Father the Nurturer rather than just Father the Provider enables a man to fully feel and express his humanity and his masculinity. Fathering is the most masculine thing a man can do." Today we give thanks for such men, including Joseph the carpenter.

Chapter 5

Christmas Eve

I have chosen to share with you the message I wrote in 2012, just a week following the massacre of elementary school children in Newtown, Connecticut. It was a very hard message to write for several reasons: I was rendered silent in my grief for a number of days, and Christmas Eve 2012 had been slated to be a joyous service due to a number of baptisms and a liturgical dance.

How does one weave together the joy that comes when a number of parents have pledged to bring their children up in the knowledge of Jesus, combined with the exquisite pain we feel for parents whose children will not return to their earthly homes? It puts our faith to the test.

It is at times such as these when our inner worlds and resources are placed in a state of great flux, that we are called upon not only to calm our children, but to calm our own inner children, whom we have perhaps neglected for years or decades. Some of these inner parts were angry and blaming and seeking to fix the problem immediately and to our own liking. Perhaps we went to the Internet to rant and rage and point fingers. Some of our inner parts were hurt and overwhelmed and just wanted to withdraw to a place where we could hold a teddy bear and pull the covers over our heads. My husband told me of an older man he knows who shared with him that he had broken down in tears three times on the day after the event.

What I want to share with you today is that there is, in each of us, an inner Self that is of God. It is able to hold and contain our inner parts that seem so agitated or activated at times such as this. And at these times we must call upon this mature, loving, adult presence within us and witness to ourselves and to others, "I am here, I am listening, I care."

It doesn't take a degree in psychology to be present for another. A sweet story of a retired psychologist who lived near the Sandy Hook school tells us that. Finding six small children who had escaped the gunman sitting at the end of his driveway that fateful morning, he invited them in for a glass of juice. He ran upstairs and grabbed a lot of his grandchildren's stuffed animals and dispensed them with care. He arranged, through their bus driver, to call their parents. He said it wasn't his training as a psychologist that helped him that day—**it was being a grandparent. His presence** was his gift to the children.

Rachel Barenblat, woman rabbi who writes a blog entitled "Velveteen Rabbi," was not in a place to be physically present for the children, but she knew that God could be present to her where she was. Her beautiful message to God cries out in pain yet seeks to be of use to God and humanity: "I'm hollow, stricken like a bell. Make of my emptiness a channel for Your boundless compassion... Strengthen the hands and hearts of Your servants tasked with caring for those wounded in body and spirit. Ignite in us the unquenchable yearning to reshape our world."

"CHILD OF PEACE"

Words and music by Bob Farrell

On a night of promise long ago,
when a star announced the light of hope
To a world that knew no peace before,
the holy Child of Peace was born.
But He stirred their longings deep within,
for His kingdom knew no end.

From a place eternal high above,
the wondrous Child of Peace had come.
Child of Comfort, Child of light,
hope that drives away the night,
Touch our lives from heaven above,
O Child of Peace, we need Your love.

In a world where peace eludes us still,
where the heart exerts its will;
At a time when words of are not enough,
O Child of Peace, we need Your love.
O Man of Peace, we need Your Love.

God who only knows your need,
Come to us, O Child of Peace.

May this Child of Peace be born in each of our hearts
this very night. Amen.

Chapter 6

Epiphany

I love the concept of epiphany. It pertains to an illuminating discovery. It pertains to seeing something important in a different way. Epiphany marks the first manifestation of Jesus to the Gentiles, the non-Jews. It signals that God loves Gentiles as well as Jews—that God's plan of salvation includes the Gentiles, too. Epiphany is also much more than this—it is a celebration of the breaking down of dividing walls, the end of hostilities between groups of people.

I remember joining forces with two women in the counseling profession to give an "Advent Retreat" at our church. During that day together, I witnessed a woman having an epiphany. It had not registered with her, prior to that time, that "The Three Wise Men" were **not** Jews, but probably Zoroastrians. Yet they travelled a long way to adore the one who was to be born King of the Jews (see Matthew 2:1-12).

AS WITH GLADNESS THOSE OF OLD
New Century Hymnal

As with gladness those of old did the guiding star behold:
As with joy they hailed its light,
leading onward, beaming bright;
So, true Morning Star, may we evermore your splendor see.

Scripture tells us that King Herod summoned the wise men secretly and ascertained from them their plan to follow a star to find out "Where is he who has been born king of the Jews? For we have seen his star in the East..." King Herod would not have welcomed such a child! Upon reaching Bethlehem and after giving gifts to the child, the wise men "fell down and worshipped him." They were then warned in a dream **not** to return to King Herod with any information about the child.

What has really changed since the time of Jesus? There are still power-hungry and paranoid leaders like Herod in the world. There are still many people who believe that **their** religion is the only way. There are still many who see the accumulation of goods as the road to salvation. All of this existed then and exists now. Perhaps nothing has changed, but an eternal invitation is still extended every year as we ponder the Epiphany. It was made manifest by three men whose curiosity and hunger for wisdom allowed them to step outside the bounds of their own religious thought system and set out on a journey to "where-they-did-not-know."

Some years ago there was a Prime Minister of Israel named David Ben-Gurion. Here are a few of his words: "Before we were Americans or Russians, Israelis or Egyptians, before we were Christians or Muslims, Hindus or Jews, before we were any of the things that divide us today, we were men and women created by God. And that is the message of the great religions." To this, I say "Amen!"

"O FOR A WORLD" (v.1,2)
The New Century Hymnal

O for a world where everyone respects each other's ways,
Where love is lived and all is done with justice
and with praise.

O for a world where goods are shared and misery relieved,
Where truth is spoken, children spared, equality achieved.

Chapter 7

The Baptism of Jesus

The words of Amos, chapter 5, verse 24, took on new meanings in the twentieth century due to the work and sacrifice of a modern prophet, Rev. Dr. Martin Luther King Jr. Says Amos, often quoted by King, "But let justice roll down like waters, and righteousness like an everflowing stream."

When, in the first decade of the twenty-first century, it came time for me to write about the baptism of Jesus, I recalled a "Negro Spiritual" that had meant a lot to me at a pivotal point in my life. It is called "Victory in Jesus," and the "cleansing flood" represents the waters of baptism.

"VICTORY IN JESUS" (v.1)
Sonshine Songs and Scriptures

I heard an old, old story, how a Savior came from glory.
How He gave his life on Calvary to save a wretch like me:
I heard about his groaning, of his precious blood's atoning.
Then I repented of my sins and won the victory.

O victory in Jesus, my Savior, forever!
He sought me and bought me with his redeeming blood;
He loved me ere I knew him
And all my love is due him.
He plunged me to victory beneath the cleansing flood.

This hymn perhaps speaks of a theology to which you are unaccustomed or are uncomfortable. It is a theology of blood, a willingness to sacrifice for one's people. It is also about a personal relationship with Christ, a term we often associate with fundamentalist Christians. But it speaks to the youngest and most insecure part of every person who encounters it. "I was loved before I knew who I was. Someone was willing to suffer for me and for all people. And through my baptism, someone gave me victory over my loneliness and separation and my fear of death."

Jesus was committing his life and his will to God through his baptism. Some call this surrender. It is a big decision. And those of us who have done it find that our egos are constantly taking back the very life and will we thought we had surrendered. Be of good faith. In community, we can stand by each other regardless.

At a symbolic level, baptism also means that we are willing to become a container for both our humanity and our divinity: A container that needs a lot of testing in order to become strong. Matthew's gospel shows John the Baptizer saying, to the Jews, "I baptize you with water for repentance, but he who is coming after me is mightier than I, whose sandals I am not worthy to carry; he will baptize you with the Holy Spirit and with fire." (Matt. 3:11, RSV) You see, all men and women who are willing to suffer for their people will encounter fire. Jesus did it and Martin Luther King did it. Here are some words by Dr. King: "The Negro will only be truly free when he reaches down to the inner depths of his own being and signs with the pen and ink of assertive selfhood his own emancipation proclamation... The Negro must boldly throw off the manacles of self-abnegation and say to himself and the world: 'I am somebody. I am a person. I am a man with dignity and honor.'"

It was the very being of Dr. King who, some years back, gave me the courage to confront the workplace discrimination that the women in my area had been encountering for years. I saw Dr. King's portrait in the credit union and I realized on a deep level that this man had given his life in order to lead his people out of abuse. Like Jesus, like a Buddhist bodhisattva, like a Native American sundancer, Martin Luther King Jr. said, with his life, "I am willing to suffer for my people."

I was very ambivalent about such an undertaking. I sought counsel from a number of people whom I respected. One of my counseling professors said to me, "There are two types of people in this world: Those who are willing to suffer abuse and those who are not." My spiritual director asked me, "How would you feel at the end of your life if you took this action, and how would you feel if you did not?" The answer was immediate: I would feel like a coward if I did not act.

I am pleased to tell you that after the ordeal I encountered, including a hearing with a federal judge from the Equal Employment Opportunity Commission, I did prevail in demonstrating the very real nature of the discrimination I had encountered. For me, it was a victory.

Chapter 8

The Calling of the Disciples

I sit quietly in our study, gazing out the window and wondering what really transpired that day by the Sea of Galilee. Matthew tells the story well into the fourth chapter of that Gospel: "Follow me, and I will make you fish for people." (vs. 19 NRSV) I am pondering what could be going on with Jesus, Peter and Andrew, James and John, that the fisherman brothers could just walk away from what they knew. I think that if we were honest with ourselves, many of us would admit that we have had fantasies of just walking away from our known, ordinary lives. But how many of us have ever done it, really started again from scratch?

My musings take me back to a workshop I attended just prior to writing this message. It was on the topic of the Myers-Briggs personality preference test. I wonder how these earliest disciples would have scored on such a thing. I recall that I became aware once again that Mr. Bolson and I are polar opposites on every one of the four indices. He is more active, I am more reflective. He is more practical, I am more imaginative. He is of the head, I am of the heart. He is decisive, I am dreamy. It was this last pairing that caught my attention in regard to the early disciples. They needed both attributes. They needed to be decisive in order to just walk away from being fishermen. And they needed to have dreams of a better life, a more meaningful life, or they simply would not have bothered. In the words of one sermon writer,

"We do not easily change the directions of our lives unless we are dissatisfied with life as it is and hopeful about what it might be."

"JESUS CALLS US, O'ER THE TUMULT" (v.1,3)
The New Century Hymnal

Jesus calls us, o'er the tumult of our life's wild, restless sea;
Day by day that voice still calls us, saying,
"Christian, follow me."
Jesus calls us from the worship of the treasures we adore,
From each idol that would keep us,
saying, "Christian, love me more."

I think that two of the most useful tools any person can carry through life are a knife and a flint. I'll bet those early fishermen carried both. The knife symbolically represents the ability to take quick action, to separate the truth from the lie, the ability to be decisive and to cut away that which does not serve us. The flint represents the capacity to produce fire. Fire can provide warmth, can change raw food into cooked food, can galvanize metal, can galvanize the will. Staring into the fire gives the dreamer time to think. Using a knife to gut a fish gives the decider a quick meal. These men needed both attributes. They needed their dreaming and dissatisfaction, and they needed their decisiveness and will. And, of course, they needed an invitation.

It is safe to say that people who are quite satisfied with their lives and their world are not ripe for change, or for leaps of faith such as those taken by the first disciples. One of the key issues a therapist always assesses is "motivation for change." Usually pain is our strongest motivation for change. Yet we today have become highly skilled at avoiding our pain. We medicate it with alcohol, food, television, drama, gambling, sex, or any of a myriad of attempted solutions. I believe that any addiction is just that: an attempted solution for existential pain.

Modern spiritual teacher Marianne Williamson once wrote a book entitled *The Gift of Change*. Here are some of her wise words:

> We seem to have great resistance to looking at our lives, and our world, with emotional honesty. And I think we are avoiding more than pain. We are avoiding the sense of hopelessness we think we feel when confronted by the enormity of the forces that obstruct us. Yet, in fact, it's when we face the darkness squarely in the eye—in ourselves and in the world—that we begin at last to see the light. And that is the alchemy of personal transformation. In the midst of the deepest, darkest night, when we feel the most humbled by life, the faint shadow of our wings begins to appear. Only when we have faced the limits of what we can do, does it begin to dawn on us the limitlessness of what God can do.

Jesus will teach these dreamy yet decisive men what it means to know themselves as men and as spirit. He and the Holy Spirit will walk with them through the darkest night of their souls, the one following the death of his body on the cross. Jesus offered the first disciples a chance to become more than fishermen. He gives us the same opportunity. This is the essence of discipleship, and I think Williamson says it well: "It is time to die to who we used to be and to become instead who we are capable of being. That is the gift that awaits us now: The chance to become who we really are." And that, of course, is children of the light.

Chapter 9

Jesus Returns to His Hometown

There is a very dramatic story found in Luke 4:14-30. In this passage, Jesus, who had been gone from his hometown of Nazareth for many years, comes home to announce to his former neighbors that the words of their Hebrew scriptures have been fulfilled in HIM. He claims the words of the prophet Isaiah and tells them, "The Spirit of the Lord is upon me, because he has anointed me to bring good news to the poor. He has sent me to proclaim release to the captives and recovery of sight to the blind, to let the oppressed go free, to proclaim the year of the Lord's favor." In modern times he probably would have been labeled psychotic, having delusions of grandeur. He was not well received, and those who heard him conspired to throw him off a cliff!

Perhaps they went home and asked themselves, "Who does Jesus think he is, and where has he been for almost two decades?" It seems plausible to me that he was somewhere studying with spiritual leaders who could help him to discover and shape the amazing person he was to become.

Think about it for a moment. What must have happened in Jesus' life to give him the courage to announce his ministry so boldly? What must have happened in his life for him to be able to heal people by his presence, sometimes without even touching them? How was he fashioned into the conduit of the Holy Spirit? The first words of the scripture passage quoted above are, "Then Jesus, filled with **the power**

of the Spirit, returned to Galilee..." (and Nazareth).

His mission was to serve the poor, the captives, the blind, the oppressed:

"GOD OF CHANGE AND GLORY" (v.1)
The New Century Hymnal

God of change and glory, God of time and space,
When we fear the future, give to us your grace.
In the midst of changing ways
Give us still the grace to praise.
Many gifts, one Spirit, one love known in many ways.
In our difference is blessing, from diversity we praise
One Giver, one Word, one Spirit, one God
Known in many ways, hallowing our days.
For the Giver, for the gifts, praise, praise, praise.

I, for one, do not believe that a cosmic God waved a magic wand and made Jesus a healer. I believe that he learned how to heal himself and thus how to heal others. We can ask ourselves, when feeling shamed, rejected or inferior, "What do you need?" We can extend warmth and presence to ourselves. We can tell the inner parts of ourselves that seem so distressed, "I can hold you, contain you. You are safe." I don't think Jesus was immune from the hurts of this world, for he had transcended his ego, the part of all people that wants to put ourselves first.

Chapter 10

Jesus' Healing Ministry

The first chapter of the book of Mark gives us a good introduction to the many acts of healing that Jesus performed. In that sickness and loss of health have been, throughout history, a reminder of our mortality and thus a source of fear, news of anyone or anything that heals us travels fast. We are told that Peter's mother-in-law was sick with a fever and that Jesus took her by the hand and lifted her up. And the fever left her.

By that evening "the whole city was gathered around the door." By morning, Jesus had to depart and go to a deserted place and pray. The disciples found him and said, "Everyone is searching for you." Jesus, however, did not let his disciples set his agenda. That came from God. He was to be a preacher and teacher of the good news of free grace, the abundant love and forgiveness of God.

Perhaps you have had a job or responsibility in which others tried to impress upon you a sense of "urgency" or "immediacy." This can be toxic for the soul. I have an idea of what Jesus might have prayed when he escaped the crowd and went out to that deserted place. It is what we call "The Lord's Prayer," but I would like to share it with you as I found it in *Prayers of the Cosmos* by a Sufi man named Neil Douglas-Klotz:

O Birther of the Cosmos, you have created all that moves in light. Focus your light within me—make me useful: Create your reign of unity now—Your one desire then acts with ours. Grant me each day what I need in bread and insight. Loose in me any regrets about myself so that I may then release others through forgiveness. Don't let surface things delude me. Free me from whatever holds me back. From you is born power and renewal. Your song beautifies all, from age to age it renews. Continue to be the Ground from which all my actions grow. Ameyn.

After Jesus prayed with words, I believe he sat calmly inhaling "ruah" or "pneuma," which are the Hebrew and the Greek words for Spirit, the breath of the Divine. For "In the beginning, God created the heavens and the earth. The earth was without form and void, and darkness was upon the face of the deep; and the Spirit of God was moving over the face of the waters." I believe he sat passively, as a tea bag in warm water, soaking in the love of God, and infusing the Divine with his own essence, his own gifts, his own life. He didn't jump up to **do something.** He sat, he breathed, and he remembered who he was: a manifestation of God.

"HERE, SAVIOR, IN THIS QUIET PLACE" (v.1)
The New Century Hymnal

Here, Savior, in this quiet place, where anyone may kneel,
I also come to ask for grace, believing you can heal.

Modern people seem to be very frenzied and filled with immediacy, like the disciples who were anxious to hit the road again with the "Jesus heals" show. The modern writer Wayne Muller posits, "In the relentless busyness of modern life, we have lost the rhythm between work and rest." He goes on to say that "our lack of rest and reflection is not just a personal affliction. It colors the way in which we build and sustain community, it dictates the way we respond to suffering, and it shapes the ways in which we seek peace and healing in the world....With a few notable exceptions the way problems are solved is frantically, desperately, reactively and badly." As Brother David Steindl-Rast reminds us, the Chinese pictograph for "busy" is composed of two characters, *heart* and *killing*.

It has been said that "No one ever died of hard work," yet we know that overwork can cause death. In Japan, *keroshi*, or "death from overwork," typically affects men between the ages of forty and fifty who work twelve to sixteen hours a day. With no previous health problems, two-thirds of these men die of brain hemorrhages and one-third from heart attacks. Overthinking, overworking, overdoing. Heart-killing.

It occurs to me that if Jesus had complied with the disciples' sense of urgency to heal others quickly, immediately and without rest, he might have died from *keroshi*. But he knew the importance of sacred rest and renewal and connection to his Source.

Chapter 11

Healing and Forgiveness

It has been very good for me, some years into my retirement, to review some of my earlier writings. This week, as I continued to read about Jesus' healing ministry, I found some words that lifted my spirit once again. One segment of the sermon was about Alcoholics Anonymous, and how the founder, Bill W., came to realize that he could not heal without the help of a Higher Power and that he needed to confess his defects to another person and then ask God to forgive them, to remove them.

I also mentioned a tragedy that occurred in our nation in 2006, when a man opened fire on some Amish school girls in Nickel Mines, Pensylvania. Ten were shot and five died. The Amish folks of that area came together to examine their faith, and to realize that they wished to extend forgiveness to the shooter. How many of us could do that?

"AMAZING GRACE, HOW SWEET THE SOUND" (v.1,3)
The New Century Hymnal

Amazing Grace, how sweet the sound,
that saved a wretch like me.
I once was lost, but now am found, was blind but now I see.
Through many dangers, toils and snares have already come.
'Tis grace has brought me safe thus far,
and grace will lead me home.

I wrote as well about a foundation that I felt called to work with, called "Soldier's Heart." I spoke a number of times with Paula Griffin of the staff. I noted that her emails ended with this statement from Thich Nhat Hanh: "Veterans are the light at the tip of the candle, illuminating the way for the whole nation. If veterans can achieve awareness, transformation, understanding and peace, they can share with the rest of society the realities of war. And they can teach us how to make peace with ourselves and each other, so we never have to use violence to resolve conflicts again."

Perhaps you remember that famous photo of a young girl in Vietnam, naked, running toward the camera. She was screaming. She had torn off her clothes, which were on fire. She had encountered the effects of the chemical napalm. The dropping of this napalm was cleared by an American, John Plummer, who had been assured and double-assured that there were no civilians in the area.

After the little girl spent more than a year in a Saigon hospital, and had endured 17 surgeries, she was able to return home. John Plummer finished his tour and went home as well, but his soul was scarred by this incident. Ten years after her injury, Phan Thi Kim Phuc became a Christian. She eventually married and was later granted asylum in Canada. John Plummer became a Christian as well, ten years after Kim did, and he felt a call to ministry, perhaps to cleanse his soul.

In 1996, Plummer learned that Kim was scheduled to speak at the Vietnam Memorial in Washington, D.C. on Veterans Day, so he decided to attend. He heard her say that she hoped someday to meet the pilot of the plane that dropped the napalm. She wanted to offer him her forgiveness. Plummer got word to her that he was in the audience. They met and embraced. She did indeed forgive him.

Is there someone from whom you would like to ask for forgiveness? What guilt is weighing you down? What shame is draining the joy from your days? What fault is causing you to limp through your life? Ask God to forgive you. God will. Then ask God for guidance in approaching the person whom you have wronged. Then go to that person in a repentant spirit and ask forgiveness. Then leave it in God's hands. You will have "cleaned up your side of the street." And you will have embarked on the path to restoration.

Chapter 12

The Beatitudes for Today

If you have a Bible where you are, you might read the passage known as "The Beatitudes," which is found in Matthew 5:1-12. Jesus recounts for a gathered crowd the many
blessings of God. Then read some powerful words from a
prophet found in Micah 6:6-8.

When I was a psychotherapist, there was a form of therapy being born called "narrative therapy." Its basic premise
is that the stories we tell ourselves about who we are become
our reality. And its second premise is that we have the power
and the right to change our narrative.

In the Micah reading, we have a prophet urging his
people to remember the very simple foundations of their
faith, for they seem to have forgotten their story, and in doing so, have forgotten their saving God. In previous verses
God reminds them of their safe delivery from slavery. Yet
the people, in their present misery, want to know how to ap-
pease God. Shall we bow down, bring burnt offerings, send
rams or rivers of oil? Shall we sacrifice our firstborn children? To which the prophet replies, **"What does the Lord
require of you but to do justice, and to love kindness, and
to walk humbly with your God?"**

Justice is identified with the nature of God. It is a virtue
that seeks to establish or restore community. It balances personal good with the common good. Kindness involves affection for and love of neighbor. Walking humbly with God

implies reverence and willingness to be taught, coupled with integrity, candor and honesty.

I'd like to recommend Roland Merullo's book *American Savior*, in which Jesus returns to run for President of the United States. The story is narrated by a very cynical journalist who is asked by Jesus to be his chief of security for the campaign. In one poignant conversation, Jesus is trying to help the journalist push through his thought patterns and his negative narrative. Kind of like Micah was trying to do with the Israelites. The reporter listens to Jesus and then asks, "And that's what you came to earth to teach us? This time, I mean? That's what you are going to do as president, make the country more... tolerant, for lack of a better word? Kinder and gentler?"

Jesus responds, "The important thing is to push down the barriers at the border of your thought patterns, to go beyond labels. I have come to help you—all of you—do that." Jesus taught the cynic to learn to inhabit the psychic space of another soul, to fully understand another. He tells the journalist that the ability to do this always results in **wise kindness.**

"LOVE DIVINE, ALL LOVES EXCELLING" (v.1)
Chalice Hymnal

Love divine, all loves excelling, joy of heaven,
to earth come down;
Fix in us thy humble dwelling,
all thy faithful mercies crown;
Jesus, thou art all compassion, pure, unbounded love thou art;
Visit us with thy salvation, enter every trembling heart.

Now let us move with courage to our passage from Matthew known as the Beatitudes, or blessings. The preaching of these statements may have caused as much harm in history as they have produced good. It is far too easy for any pastor to preach the beatitudes as if they were injunctions. To say, for instance, that you must be poor in spirit, you must mourn, you must be meek, and so forth. As one interpreter said, "Who can survive in attempting to live into the spirit of the beatitudes?" That author will eventually tell us that there are three principles for living into the spirit of the beatitudes: simplicity, hopefulness and compassion.

The first hearers of the beatitudes would have seen and heard things familiar to them. Jesus went up on a mountain: This would have been an allusion to Moses. Jesus could be seen as "the new Moses" who hands down not the ten commandments, but the beatitudes, God's blessings. They would have heard the words of Isaiah in the teachings of Jesus, especially as found in the 61st chapter of that prophet. For they would hear again of the proclamation of the good news to the poor, of the comforting of all those who mourn, and the healing of the brokenhearted.

These words were given for the sake of encouragement. You see, finding one's self in the midst of oppression invites the invasion of negative thoughts. "Why is God doing this to me?" "How can God allow this type of person to rule me?" You can easily see how the narrative becomes tainted. By entertaining these thoughts, I separate myself from God and my fellow human beings. I become lonely and afraid.

One commentator gave me some excellent advice. He

said to focus on one beatitude in order to avoid overwhelming oneself. To this end, I'd like to speak to the sixth beatitude, "Blessed are the pure in heart for they shall see God." I'm fond of the interpretation of this phrase found in Glenda Green's book *Love Without End: Jesus Speaks*. In Green's book, Jesus states, "In the eyes of God, who knows nothing of sin, you are nothing less than perfect.... In the purity of your heart you are one with your Creator." Jesus is asked why we do not enter our hearts more easily. He responds, "Because you do not see yourself as pure, perfect and innocent. As long as you try to carry all of your unworthiness and mistakes (into your heart) with you, you will stay at the threshold of your heart and not enter."

Do you see yourself as defective? Please let Jesus be your game changer, your narrative changer. Amen.

Chapter 13

Paul and the Corinthians

For those who do not know him, let me introduce you to the "Apostle Paul." Why, you may wonder, is he not called one of the disciples? Paul was not a fisherman enlisted by Jesus on the seashore. He was a very strict Jewish man of high birth who was persecuting Christians! But one day, on the road to Damascus, he had a very dramatic conversion experience to Christianity and became a significant voice as an evangelist. Much of the New Testament was written by Paul, most generally in the form of letters to the various churches he served.

I am so grateful for the life and writings of the Apostle Paul. For a long time I held a grudge against him because of his positions on women. But a burden was lifted for me when I realized that like everyone else, he was a product of his time and culture. He had his own fish to fry that we never even have to think about in our time and culture. When was the last time you argued about circumcision or whether people could eat food that was offered to idols or whether women should wear veils to prophesy? Paul had to deal with all of that.

One of the churches that Paul served was in Corinth. It was a contentious community. One of the issues that irked the Corinthians was that Paul asked them to financially support the church in Jerusalem. What?! The "weak" give to the "strong?" I smile as I think about how church finances have always been a sore issue with members. One scholar named L.T. Johnson described the church in Corinth as "a community whose life together was a mixture of confusion, pettiness and ambition, as well as enthusiasm and fervor."

Corinth was a port city with a large transient population that brought in various cults. There was a synagogue and a shrine to Isis. Corinth was the site of the famous Isthmian games, something akin to the Olympics. Paul utilized this fact to make a point: "Do you not know that in a race the runners all compete, but only one receives the prize? Run in such a way that you may win it. Athletes exercise self-control in all things; they do it to receive a perishable wreath, but we an imperishable one." There are many dedicated athletes in my mountain community. Paul was dedicated in his ministry.

Here are a few words from an African-American spiritual that are still popular today:

"Guide My Feet"
The New Century Hymnal

Guide my feet while I run this race,
guide my feet while I run this race,
Guide my feet while I run this race,
For I don't want to run this race in vain.

A number of years ago, some relatives invited us to attend an Air Force Academy football game in Colorado Springs. I am not a football fan. I don't understand the game; I don't care for the violence that leaves many players disabled sooner or later. I almost begged off the invitation, but something inside me urged me on.

At these games, whenever Air Force scores, the first-year cadets are required to vacate their seats, run down to the playing field and perform the number of pushups that matches the Air Force score. By the time the game was over, the cadets were pumping out 53 pushups. I pondered this whole phenomenon for quite a while. I finally determined that the reason I was at that game was to witness with my own eyes the fruits of **discipline.**

I don't envision Paul dropping down for 53 pushups at a football game, but I do see him praying, and holding his tongue, and reaching out everywhere to establish that "one great fellowship of God, throughout the whole wide world." It was tough to do this when his own beloved congregations were as fractious as the Corinthians.

Thank you, Paul, for your discipline and commitment, and for keeping your eyes on the prize. Amen.

Chapter 14

Radiance

The Christian year has been divided into a number of seasons. After Christmas, there comes a season of "Epiphany" that celebrates the making known of Jesus to the Magi or Wise Men. The next season is Lent, the weeks before Easter. But there is one Sunday tucked in the middle, and it is called "The Transfiguration." The name comes from an experience of Peter, James and John, whom Jesus took with him up to a mountain to pray. There, Jesus became radiant dazzling white and was joined by Moses and Elijah. The disciples were admonished by God to listen to his Son Jesus. This encounter is found in Luke 9:28-36.

This passage has often been compared to that of Moses, who met God on Mount Sinai. Paul speaks of it in one of his letters to the church in Corinth. Paul had, himself, encountered radiant light when he met the risen Christ on the road to Damascus. In fact, that light blinded him for several days. Yes, Paul understood "radiance," and he understood metanoia, a changing of one's heart and mind. For Paul had been a very legalistic Jew who clamored to destroy Christianity. His experience with Jesus led him to reexamine some of his beliefs. He began to experience the Ten Commandments as a form of legalism, which implies that unless we are being good, law-abiding citizens, we cannot know God. In place of legalism, Paul would develop a theology of grace wherein forgiveness is always offered to those who sin if they will but take it.

The beloved hymn "Amazing Grace" was penned by a man who experienced a similar change of heart and mind. John Newton was a slave trader who came to see the error of his ways. He had a remarkable conversion and accepted God's grace. "I once was blind, but now I see" he wrote in that hymn. For the grace of God released him from the bondage of sin and brought sight to his eyes. His hard heart was softened. His "blind" eyes gained sight.

Radiance is not found only in saints or those who will be sainted. I once read a story about a six-year-old who conveyed radiance to his congregation. This happened in a black church worship service, where God's presence in community is experienced, perhaps through shared smiles, warm greetings, fervent prayer, soul-stirring gospel music, hand clapping, shouts of praise and amens. This lad was restless. He turned around and saw radiant smiles on the people behind him. And a broad glowing smile appeared on his face as well. This form of radiance spreads among people.

I had an experience somewhat like this when I was living in Chicago a while back. I took it upon myself to visit a lot of Twelve-Step programs in the area near the seminary I was attending. On a particular Friday night, I had hiked fairly far to a church and I walked down the steps to the basement. There was a young man dancing about the room putting up chairs, setting up the coffee maker, and singing. He was radiant. He told me, with a contagious smile on his face, that he was "just a foot soldier in God's army." I recognized before me a man who was in the midst of a spiritual awakening. Twelve-Step literature tells us that such a person has now become able to do, feel, and believe that which he could not do before on his unaided strength and resources alone. "He finds himself in possession of a degree of honesty, tolerance, unselfishness, peace of mind, and love of which he had thought himself quite incapable. What he has received is a free gift, and yet usually, at least in some small part, he has made himself ready to receive it."

You see, spiritual awakening is not just available to people like Moses or Jesus or Paul. It is available to everyone. I'll close with an image from the world of art. It was written about by Thomas Currie in a series of books entitled *Feasting on the Word*. He speaks of one of Vincent van Gogh's paintings. This one shows a pair of old, worn-out work boots. They seem very "ordinary and inglorious." But a closer look shows that the boots are illumined "and that they describe a life not just of labor and toil, but of vast human dignity, even beauty... These boots cry out that their owner was made for the glory of God, that to be a human being is to be a glory-bearing, glory-reflecting, glory-bound creature." Currie reminds us that the famous theologian Karl Barth has referred to the risen Lord as "the one who makes us radiant."

"O RADIANT CHRIST, INCARNATE WORD"
The New Century Hymnal

O Radiant Christ, incarnate Word,
eternal love, revealed in time:
Come, make your home within our hearts,
that we may dwell
In light sublime.

Chapter 15

What is Lent?

The season of Lent begins with the promises God made to some of our oldest ancestors: Noah, Abraham, Sarah and Moses. Through them and others, we glimpse what it means to live as a righteous person. We rejoice along with these ancestors that God desires to save and heal, and to continue to deliver all people.

The word "Lent" comes from the anglo-Saxon word meaning "spring" or "springtime." It is the time of year, in the northern hemisphere, when the days begin to lengthen. What was cold becomes warm; what was dormant springs into newness. Just as the hidden bulb breaks through the winter earth, so the church stirs into action to proclaim the Easter mystery: In dying, God destroyed death and in rising, God is restoring life all around us!

"IN THE BULB THERE IS A FLOWER"
The New Century Hymnal

In the bulb there is a flower; in the seed, an apple tree;
In cocoons, a hidden promise: butterflies will soon be free!
In the cold and snow of winter,
there's a spring that waits to be,
Unrevealed until its season, something God alone can see.

One of my colleagues during graduate school went on to become a pastor in Boston. Liz Myer Boulton reported in one of her church newsletters that there is a community-based reason why **fasting** is encouraged during Lent. She explained that in the agrarian calendar, foodstores are traditionally low in the early spring. Perhaps the root vegetables and grains put away at harvest time have been largely consumed. Therefore, Lenten fasting has its origins in the rhythm of nature. Holding a fast together was the only way a community could preserve the lives of all its members. Today, however, fasting is more of a choice than a necessity. Liz suggests that during the 40 days of Lent, we choose to limit our consumption of the world's resources. "Let's generate less waste and allow restraint to replace gratification."

Almsgiving is another Christian practice associated with Lent. It is a perfect time to consider giving more time, money and effort to feeding the hungry, visiting the lonely, and restoring dignity and justice to people everywhere. Liz wrote, "Lent is a season of birthing, plowing and sowing. Let's sow ourselves generously for the next forty days and attempt to right the wrongs that unequal distribution of wealth and power have caused."

The third practice associated with Lent is **prayer.** Prayer takes many forms in our modern culture. Some forms of prayer include heavy, sonorous, lengthy beseeching to God to make us better people. Other forms of prayer include training the busy and active mind of the one who prays to become still, to know that God is surely with us. And perhaps this form of stillness allows God to get a word in edgewise! Those of a Buddhist persuasion have a term called "Monkey Mind." This is the constant chatter in our thoughts that we so often allow. When we can become present in the moment, the projections and fears clouding our windows of perception begin to dissolve. We begin to see with new eyes. These words of wisdom come from a spiritual leader named Isha, who penned a small book entitled *Why Walk When You Can Fly?* I have worked with this practice for many years.

The scripture readings most commonly associated with Lent pertain to the forty days and nights that Jesus is said to have spent in the wilderness being tested by Satan. The figure known as Satan is not a man in a red union suit carrying a pitchfork. Clarence Jordan suggests in *The Substance of Faith* that the Greek word *diablos*, which we translate as devil, comes from *dia*, meaning "around through" and *bollo*, meaning "to throw." Our English word for ball comes from *bollo*. Diablos therefore means "one who throws things about"—one who stirs things up and gets things confused. The work of "the devil" therefore is to get us muddled. The devil then, is really the Great Confuser, who wants Jesus and all of us to forget who we really are. These words come from writer Bill Wylie-Kellerman:

> I submit to you this Lenten season, that you do not need to worry about how you will make manifest the love of God that is within you. The Holy Spirit will make that known to you if you will wait and listen in silence, without an agenda. We must "unplug" from social media, from advertising, from news reports for a portion of every day.

I'll close with more words from Wylie-Kellerman:

> To keep Lent is to discover and remember who in heaven's name we are, as a person and community. We pray against all confusers and confusions for our true identity and vocation. We know that this means standing before the cross and making some choices. The grace of this season is that Jesus suffers the choice with us. Let the further grace be that we make our choices as disciples, in the mind and heart of Christ.

Amen.

Chapter 16

Nicodemus and Life in the Spirit

In the third chapter of the book of John, we meet a Jewish leader named Nicodemus who sought Jesus out in the night, so as not to be seen by other Jews. He was a Pharisee, a keeper of the law. But he was very drawn to Jesus' teachings. In modern terms, we might say that Jesus had a bit of "cognitive restructuring" to do with Nicodemus before the concept of life in the Spirit could be understood.

Let me give you an example. Let's say that next week you become lost in your thoughts while driving your car and you begin to exceed the speed limit. Before long there are flashing lights and the sound of a siren. You pull over and are greeted by a highway patrol officer. Perhaps you shake your head in remorse, but you hand over your driver's license and accept the citation and payment envelope. Another person might react quite differently due to his or her thought patterns. This person's mind might go immediately to themes of persecution, angry thoughts and desire for revenge. "Doesn't that stupid cop have anything better to do? They are all out to get me. It has been like this my whole life," fumes the individual. He/she plans to locate the vehicle the officer is driving while it is in the lot and then slash the tires.

What is the difference in these two incidents? **It is merely the thoughts of the speeder.** And the behaviors that follow them. This is the essence of cognitive restructuring, to find and change old thought patterns. Jesus is trying to effect this in the mind of Nicodemus, who, though a spiritual leader, is actually fairly clueless about life in the Spirit. Jesus speaks to him of being born anew, this time in the Spirit, and Nicodemus initially cannot get past trying to think his way out of re-entering his mother's womb to be physically born again. Jesus wanted Nicodemus to be able to remember his life before he became form, to remember his life when he dwelt in God, or Unity.

One early Jewish mystical practice used before and at the time of Jesus involved remembering and re-experiencing the creation story in one's own being. The original archetype of Adam, the first person, the perfection of humanity, became a focus for meditation. One could experience the process of the light entering the darkness not simply as a mythic story, but also in one's own awareness. Thus, one could become "born again," just as human consciousness was born in Adam, that point in history when God-consciousness was born in humans.

These clues show that Jesus wanted Nicodemus to recreate the creation story within himself. A Buddhist might accomplish this by pondering the koan: "Where were you before your grandparents were born?" Early Jewish mystical practices encouraged practitioners to try to re-experience the descent of **spirit and breath** into form, and then experience resurrection and ascension in a journey back to the Holy One. I believe that Jesus wanted Nicodemus to experience all of this in order to reduce his fear of death, which colors all of one's perceptions. Nicodemus would later argue for a fair legal hearing for Jesus, and he brought expensive oils and spices for Jesus' embalming. He was present at the crucifixion and saw this lack of fear in Jesus.

"BREATHE ON ME, BREATH OF GOD"
The New Century Hymnal

Breathe on Me, Breath of God,
fill me with life anew
That I may love the way you love
and do what you would do.

Today I applaud the curiosity and courage of the Pharisee Nicodemus, and I thank God for his conversion to Life in the Spirit.

Chapter 17

Jesus and the Money Changers

I am smiling this morning as I type, for many of these words came to me from a retired minister named Dick Donovan, who began an online service for pastors called "Sermon Writer." One of Dick's favorite sermon writers was a man named Rev. Charles Hoffacker. For the words I share this day, I owe them each a debt of gratitude.

Gods come in different sizes. Lent is a good time to consider the size of the God we serve. Do you remember Michael Milken? In 1989 his name was often in the news. It was he who created, almost single-handedly, the junk bond market that spawned the takeover craze that destroyed some organizations and saddled others with tremendous debt.

For a long while, Michael Milken did quite well for himself. He was a billionaire before he turned forty. But eventually he found himself at the center of the biggest fraud investigation in Wall Street history. He pleaded guilty to six felony counts. His sentence included more that a half billion dollars in fines as well as a lengthy prison sentence.

Milken's downfall was not due to any lack of effort on his part. He was clever and energetic, willing to risk again and again. The problem lay elsewhere. His god was too small. He had made an idol out of Wealth, and it became his god, to whom he was devoted. This devotion led him to steal. Unfortunately, safeguards were so ineffective that his actions had a devastating effect on the national economy and on the lives and fortunes of thousands of people.

Michael Milken had big dreams, and exerted tremendous efforts to realize them, but the god he served was too small, and so Milken became very small as well. As he stood in federal court at the conclusion of his trial, he expressed no regret over the damage he had done to many lives.

We are wrong if we see our current times with a "shortage of belief." There is no shortage today. There is considerable belief, today as always, in gods that are not gods, in gods that are idols, in gods that are too small. These idols are potent, however, for they reduce the stature of whomever worships them.

The Ten Commandments, those laws given by God through Moses, constitute a series of warnings against the most popular small gods. For example, the Sabbath command warns us against the small god of Work, whose worshippers resort to frenetic activity in order to feel they have a right to exist.

The commandment against murder warns us against making our Enemy into an idol, for strangely enough, that is what happens when hate comes to rule our life, for our opponent becomes our obsession.

On the other hand, the commandment against coveting warns us against making our Neighbor into an idol, a small god, for that happens when we regard something our neighbor has as indispensable for our existence.

The Ten Commandments are not simply law in the usual sense, concerned with what is right and wrong. These commandments are about loyalty, our loyalty to a true God instead of idols, or false gods. The God of all ages comes to set us free.

We see this liberation take place when Jesus causes an uproar in the temple at Jerusalem. In he goes one day, brandishing a handmade whip, and he starts making trouble! Animals stampede, angry merchants shout, tables are overturned and coins are rolling about everywhere. The temple court, turned by Caiaphas into a street bazaar, is reduced to mayhem.

What prompted Jesus? It was that the money changers and merchants had made Profit their god. They had obscured the temple's purpose as a house of prayer for all people. It was turning into a location of service to small gods. No wonder Jesus is angry!

Jesus sees that our hearts can become such small temples, housing small gods. Through the Ten Commandments, through our study of his life and words, through our prayers and supplication he comes to us, eager to re-consecrate the temple of our lives.

"God of Grace and God of Glory"
The New Century Hymnal

God of Grace and God of Glory,
on your people pour your power;
Crown your ancient church's story;
bring its bud to glorious flower.
Grant us wisdom, grant us courage,
for the facing of this hour,
For the facing of this hour.

Chapter 18

Of Life and Death and Life Again

The story of Jesus raising Lazarus from the dead is found in the eleventh chapter of John, my favorite gospel writer. The other three writers tell the same narrative, but the Gospel of John seems more mystical and loving. In the eleventh chapter, Jesus has received word that his dear friend Lazarus is ill. Lazarus' sisters, also beloved friends of Jesus, send word to him. Jesus elects to stay in the town where he has been, and Lazarus dies. The sisters are wild with grief, and as so often happens in hospices and hospitals today, they lash out at those whom they expected to prevent the death of their loved one. They berate Jesus when he does arrive, saying, "If you had been here my brother would not have died."

My heart goes out to Mary and Martha, the sisters. I have seen people lash out in fear and grief. I have been that person. John O'Donohue says, "Death is a lonely visitor. After it visits your home, nothing is ever the same again. There is an empty place at the table; there is an absence in the house. (It) is an incredibly strange and lonely experience." Jesus meets these grieving women with the statement that Lazarus will rise again. They reply that they know this will happen at the resurrection. Jesus gives them a surprising response. He tells them that **he is the resurrection**, that everyone who believes in him, though they die, will live. Jesus brings Lazarus back to life.

I once attended a workshop led by Frank Ostaseski,

who had founded the Zen Hospice in San Francisco a number of years previously. He gathered up the homeless people who were dying alone in seedy hotels and shelters and gave them clean, loving and sacred spaces in which to make their passage.

A film crew showed up one day and asked if they could film him talking to someone about their impending death. At first, Frank sent them away, thinking that their request was very intrusive. Then one of his intake workers told him about a most incredible woman who was signing in, and who was more than willing to talk about her process on film.

She was an immigrant from Asia. She had had cancer for seven years and was accepting that she would not overcome it. She had been a practicing Buddhist for twelve years, but had more recently been influenced by Christianity. One of the things she talked about was forgiveness. It seems that her family of origin had disowned her both by telephone and in a letter. She had lived with a man who was abusive. She had been a street person for several years. She had found the life of Christ to be transforming for her. I am sure she identified with his crucifixion. The part that amazed her so were his words, "Father, forgive them, for they know not what they do." She felt that if Jesus could forgive this atrocious and unfair cruelty, she could, too. She said, "I just wanted to love again." *A Course in Miracles* tells us that our only function in this life is to forgive. I saw the fruits of that function in this radiant woman. I was so humbled.

"My Life Flows on in Endless Song" (v.2)
The New Century Hymnal

What though my joys and comforts die?
My Savior still is living.
What though the shadows gather round?
A new song Christ is giving.
No storm can shake my inmost calm,
while to that Rock I'm clinging;
Since Love commands both heaven and earth,
how can I keep from singing?

Chapter 19

Stay Awake

A number of years ago, I began my Palm Sunday message with some observations I'd made following a discussion with various clergy in my small community. We wrestled with the question "what are scriptures?" Some folks believe they are indisputable, the "letter of the law." I stated that I do not believe in "the inerrancy of scripture," as do many in the denomination I served. I wrote, "We believe that much of what is in the Bible is God-inspired, but we also know that it was written and translated by human beings at various points in their own journeys and in the journeys of their people." Someone else mentioned that God did not quit communicating with humans when the books of the New Testament were selected and written down as canon. It reminded me of a good phrase: "God is still speaking."

I once spent some time in a setting where it seemed to me that the words of the Bible were more revered than God. I mentioned a phrase called "bibliolatry" where the book becomes the idol. I contrasted this with the Native American custom whereby elders share the people's stories in sacred ways, not with books but with memories. It is important to tell our stories from our hearts in the presence of our children. And the more we say them out loud, the more we claim them.

This is the week called Holy Week, when Jesus rode triumphantly into Jerusalem and was, later in the week, hung from a cross. We are asked to walk with him and his disciples every step of the way. Jesus knew that he would endure and he knew where he would go, but they did not. They loved the palm branches and cheering crowd, but in the end, they could not stay awake with him in his hour of greatest need.

Episcopal priest Barbara Brown Taylor became my "conversation partner" for the creation of this message. She reminded me that Jesus had tried in so many ways to tell the disciples of a new form of perception that did not involve the goals of this world. He didn't have a fancy house—he was a homeless, itinerant preacher. He didn't enjoy a high position in the government or culture—he rode into town on a donkey! He did not seek to control his destiny—he went to the cross alone. No one would even stay awake for him. One sold him, many denied him.

It was late and the Passover meal was sumptuous. He had washed their feet. They could not understand his request that they might stay awake with him. "Stay awake," he calls down the centuries to us. "Remember who you are. We are all of God. Love is the only thing that is real or permanent. Do not fall asleep to these notions." But we doze off into our various ego fantasies and try to outdo others rather than extend love to them.

Jesus took his awareness of our blindness with him to the garden that night. He prayed that we might all be one. He prayed for the day when sharing by all might mean scarcity for none.

"STAY WITH ME"
Songs & Prayers from Taize

Stay with me, remain here with me, watch and pray,
Watch and pray.

He was a threat to those who felt they understood God
better than he did. They, like many throughout time, enjoyed
the privilege and position to broker God to the masses. But
he would not have it. He knew that God-consciousness is in
every one of us. That we are all potential miracle workers.
That love cannot be bartered or sold. That we can only know
it if we give it away. It was as if he knew the truth about them,
and about us—that we are amateurs at love, that we do fall
asleep on him, that we fail to answer his call for our help, and
we abandon him when the going gets tough.

Yet he forgives us before we even turn away. And the
road back to him is always open. May we please walk as
far with him as we can. Let us ponder what it is that keeps
us from manifesting the God within us. May God draw us
deeper into the teachings of Jesus and help us to stay awake
to our divine inheritance, that we may be less free with our
judgment and more extravagant with our love. Amen.

Chapter 20

Easter with the Blackbird Children

I think the most courageous and compelling sermon I ever wrote was delivered on an Easter Sunday after I had read *Untie the Strong Woman* by Clarissa Pinkola Estes. Estes is a skilled "cantadora," or story-teller. I have pondered and prayed about whether I could include her work in this book I am writing. And the answer came back, "Yes, these stories need to be told."

The story about the crucifixion of Jesus is found in a chapter wherein Estes tells of a job she had many decades ago when she was 26 years old. She was a brand-new, first-time counselor and teacher of three education-in-prison classes for teenaged female prisoners. The classes were Poetry, Cooking and Human Sexuality. Her students ranged in age from 12 to 19 years. Some were of danger to themselves, some were of danger to others. They had been locked up for theft, drugs or for being chronic runaways. Many were said to be "stone-cold tough."

Estes, in her own mind, began to call these girls "the blackbird children," for they were very skittish and flapped and flapped at the slightest change in routine, facial expression, or tone of voice from others. They had homemade tattoos up and down their arms and legs, black ballpoint pen fingernails, and black lipstick. They literally turned their backs on her, cawing like crows when she suggested they begin making cinnamon rolls. They hooted, called her names and threw dough across the room.

The ways in which the young teacher transformed her relationship with these "blackbird children" are quite remarkable. The reader has already come to realize that Estes comes from a multicultural background of displaced and disregarded peoples. The reader has also come to see that one of the gifts of her tight-knit clan was a total lack of embarrassment at claiming one's faith, not only in God, but in Mary and her child Jesus. Estes has come to see Mary, the mother of Jesus, who stood at his cross and wept, as one who is always aware of and attentive to our sufferings.

Estes was close to being overwhelmed by the sufferings of the blackbird children. She could have become one of countless young teachers who, upon becoming fully immersed in prison culture, decide it is too overwhelming and simply leave. Drawing upon her faith in Mary, the mother of Jesus, she took a bold leap of faith and challenged the girls in her class to consider a handmade tattoo that almost every one of them had penned upon herself. I can't go into a lot of detail here, but it contained a word that rhymes with "clucker" and starts with the letter f. In trying to get the girls to see why this phrase was not in their best interest, she blurted out one day that she would take one letter a day from that nasty word and give that letter a more beautiful meaning than it held in the clucker-rhyming word.

From that point on she was depending on Mary every day to instruct her. One day, she walked the highway for more than two miles asking the dear Mother to tell her what in the world she could do with the letter "c." She saw miles of telephone poles along the roadside. They looked to her like the crosses at Golgotha, where Jesus was crucified.

The next day in cooking class, she drew a "c" onto the center of one of the loaves of bread that was to be baked. Over the letter she drew a large cross. She said, "This is the **Cross** on the round-topped hill called Golgotha." The girls squawked and jeered. She told them that Golgotha meant "the place of the skull." Skulls. Now she had their attention.

She told them it was a place where people who were deemed criminals were dragged off to be scourged, to hang on a cross, to not be able to leave the pain. This they understood. She softly pointed out that they were all old enough now to have experienced at least one broken heart. And that *that* was a kind of crucifixion. Something you couldn't run away from.

She told them about the God of Love being found guilty of loving humanity instead of following the orders of the rulers and authorities of His time. They understood completely being forced to follow rules instead of learning the Rules of Love. Some of the girls cried to hear that the Child of Love, who included the downtrodden in his care, had been murdered, crucified.

Estes shares that in prison, those incarcerated were not supposed to touch one another, ever, even in love. Yet in this situation, she went ahead and touched the shoulders of the weeping girls. Other girls came to comfort them as well. She spoke to them of standing together to comfort the tormented.

The blackbird children understood. No jeering or acting silly, just being quiet and truly kind. They silently moved to clean up the kitchen then, to the fragrant smell of leavened bread rising. For these girls, the love of Christ had now become personal, along with the love of Mary. Someone cared about their pain. Amen.

"NOW THE GREEN BLADE RISES" (v.4)
The New Century Hymnal

When our hearts are wintry, grieving or in pain,
Christ's warm touch can call us back to life again.
Fields of our hearts that dead and bare have been:
Love is come again like wheat that rises green.

Chapter 21

The Miracle of Understanding

I have learned a great deal from a remarkable book called *A Course in Miracles*. In this chapter is a message I penned, following closely the teachings of *The Course* regarding the meaning of the crucifixion. It speaks using the voice of Jesus.

I want you to understand that the crucifixion was the last useless journey that Humanity need take, and that it represents release from fear to anyone who understands it. Perhaps you have felt crucified in your lifetime. This is a marked tendency of those who feel separated, who always refuse to consider what they have done to themselves. Thus, they project blame and all manner of bad feelings from within themselves onto others. Yes, a body can be assaulted, but you are not a body. You are a manifestation of God and as such cannot be destroyed.

You are free to perceive yourself as persecuted if you wish. I would rather that you understand that I am like you and you are like me. I would rather that you remember that I was persecuted as the world judges and did not share this evaluation for myself. And because I did not share it, I did not strengthen it. I therefore offered a different interpretation of attack. I want you to believe it and help me teach it, for as you teach, so shall you learn.

I want you to know and to teach your own perfect immunity, which is the truth in you, and realize that it cannot be assailed. Do not try to protect your immunity or you are

believing that you are assailable. You are not asked to be crucified. That was my teaching contribution. You will be given
less extreme temptations to misperceive, and you are asked
not to accept them as false justifications for anger.

Your resurrection is your reawakening. The Holy Spirit
will instruct you in the ways of true perception. My brothers
slept during the so-called "agony in the garden," but I could
not be angry with them because I knew I could not be abandoned. I had made a decision to hear only one Voice, and
I will build my church on those who follow. A church that
does not inspire love has a hidden altar that is not serving
the purpose for which God intended it.

I elected, for your sake and mine, to demonstrate that
the most outrageous assault, as judged by the ego (the separated one) does not matter. As the world judges these things,
but not as God knows them, I was betrayed, abandoned,
beaten, torn and finally killed. It was clear that this was only
because of the projection of guilt onto me by others, since I
had not harmed anyone and had healed many.

The message of the crucifixion is very clear: Teach only
love, for that is what you are. If you use the crucifixion in
any other way you are using it for assault and not as a call
to peace. The Apostles often misunderstood it. Their own
imperfect love made them vulnerable to projection and out
of their own fear they spoke of "the wrath of God." There is
no such thing. The apostles felt guilty, or they never could
have quoted me as saying "I come not to bring peace but a
sword." This is clearly the opposite of everything I taught.
They couldn't have written so scathingly about Judas whom

they believed betrayed me. I do not and did not believe in betrayal. Judas was my brother and a Son of God, as much a part of Humanity as I am myself.

Do not be fearful as you read the teachings of the Apostles. I told them and I tell you that there is much you will understand later. I do not want you to allow any fear to enter into the thought system toward which I am guiding you. I do not call for martyrs but for teachers. No one is punished for sins, for the Sons of God are not sinners. You were created as a Creator, as was every other person. It is solely a device of the ego to make you feel different from your brothers and separated from them.

Remember that the Holy Spirit is the communication link between God the Creator and God's separated Creations. If you will listen to the Spirit's voice, you will know that you can neither hurt nor be hurt, and that many need your blessing to help them hear this for themselves. When you perceive this need for blessing in others, and do not respond to any other need, you will have learned of me, and will be as eager to share your learning as I am.

"Peace I Leave with You, My Friends"
New Century Hymnal

Peace I leave with you, my friends,
shalom my peace, in all you do.
Peace I leave with you, my friends,
I give to you so you can give to others, too.
To share God's love is why I came, to show God's kindness without end. Go now, my friends, and do the same, until I come again.

Chapter 22

Spiritual Lineage

My husband and I once had an interesting conversation with a friend from England. Steve asked her, in diplomatic ways, if she could help him understand the fascination with royalty in England. Our dear friend began her explanation. No, it was not a case of celebrity worship such as we know in America, she said. It was a connection to ancient history, which the United States in its present form does not have, she added. The word she used perhaps most often was "lineage," and she stressed what an important concept that was. It all seemed quite incomprehensible to me.

Afterwards, I thought about all of the emphasis on lineage in the Old Testament. Abraham begat Isaac begat Jacob and so on. I thought about how my beliefs in democracy and my beliefs in Christianity delivered me from belief in "biological lineage." Instead, I believe in a statement made in our Declaration of Independence: "We hold these truths to be self-evident, that all men are created equal, that they are endowed by their Creator with certain unalienable Rights, that among these are Life, Liberty and the Pursuit of Happiness." The term "men" here refers to humanity, in my way of thinking.

Jump forward now from the lineages emphasized in Judaism to the message of Jesus that we are all meant to be one. Consider his care for the disenfranchised, and for those with no "lineage" of importance. Consider how he appeared to

Mary as a common gardener outside his tomb after the crucifixion. Also during that time, he appeared to two common men walking home to Emmaus after witnessing the events that happened in Jerusalem, and the "death" of Jesus.

The travelers explained their sadness to "the stranger" on the road by saying, "We had hoped that he was the one to redeem Israel." They recounted the events of the day as they had been told to them. They urged their companion to stay with them for supper. After Jesus blessed and broke the bread, their eyes were opened and they recognized him. After he vanished, they said, "Were not our hearts burning within us while he was talking to us on the road, while he was opening the scriptures to us?"

This, dear friends, is how I measure scripture. My heart does not burn when I consider who begat whom. But it does burn when I consider the words of the author of 1 Peter that God judges all people impartially according to their deeds. It burns even brighter when this author speaks of genuine mutual love, and states, "You have been born anew, not of perishable but of imperishable seed, through the living and enduring word of God."

That author will go on to share that the good news is brought to **all of us** by the Holy Spirit sent from heaven. This news includes "things into which angels long to look." Might these words warm our hearts?

Who are your ancestors in the faith? They need not be related to you by biological lineage. If you had abusive or absent parents, you need not let that taint your life forever. We do not presently live in a world in which your parents' social station in life predicts your life. And we do not live in a world in which their behavior toward us need define us forever. We create the world we see. If we claim the spiritual lineage of Christ, we claim love, hope, possibility. We claim the imperishable seed.

"In Christ There is No East or West" (v.1)
The New Century Hymnal

In Christ there is not east or west,
in him no south or north,
But one community of love
throughout the whole wide earth.

Chapter 23

On Becoming a Shepherd

The image of Jesus as the good shepherd is very dear to me. It calms me, it fills my heart with love, I relax in the safety of his arms. In years gone by I have wept my way through the preparation of this sermon with tears of gratitude for the remembrance that I am safe, and that nothing can separate me from the love of God. Nothing, that is, but my own thinking.

Let's spend a moment locating this story in Jesus' ministry. The good shepherd theme has its origin in the story of the man born blind. Jesus healed the blind man, bringing about a controversy with Jewish religious leaders, who refused to believe that Jesus had performed a miracle. They tried to discredit Jesus. Then the formerly blind man bore testimony to Jesus. The religious leaders drove him out, though the man now had physical and spiritual sight, which the leaders refused to acknowledge.

It is important here to distinguish between a hired hand and a true shepherd. A hired hand is in the position for money. He is always looking for shortcuts. If the sheep bleats in the middle of the night, he may or may not attend to it. If wolves approach the flock, he may or may not engage them. But a true shepherd has a calling and not just a job. **Being a shepherd is not for the fainthearted.**

Jesus has taken the metaphors for the good and bad shepherds from the Old Testament prophet Ezekiel, who speaks of the religious leaders of Israel (shepherds) as those who have been feeding themselves. The prophet asks "Should not shepherds feed the sheep? You eat the fat, you clothe yourselves with the wool, you slaughter the fatlings; but you do not feed the sheep." These hired hands are not shepherds. The passage concludes with God promising Israel, "You are my sheep, the sheep of my pasture, and I am your God, says the Lord God."

And now I pose a question to you that must have weighed heavily on the hearts of the disciples during the weeks following the physical death of Jesus. **"Who will tend the flocks now?"** Put yourself in the shoes of the disciples during this period between the crucifixion and the Pentecost. Jesus realized that it was time to hand off the baton, so to speak, but the poor disciples were too bereft to recognize him.

Jesus needed his disciples to become the message he sought to teach. But one cannot give the good news of free grace if one has not received it. One cannot be the joy that God **is** without being cleansed of all those feelings the disciples felt. Thus, Jesus set out to feed the disciples, the future shepherds. "Having loved his own who were in the world, he loved them to the end." Please join me in a guided meditation on becoming a shepherd. Start by taking a few deep, cleansing breaths.

Imagine that you are a lamb. Much of the time, your life is good. Your mother is nearby. You have come to recognize the voice, the song, the whistle of the shepherd who cares for you. You feel connected to the flock. One night, you awaken and feel hungry. You decide to venture off on your own in search of something to eat. You lose your footing and tumble down a steep rock face onto a small precipice. You cry out in your little lamb voice. Never have you felt so frightened and alone. Before long the shepherd appears at the top of the rock face. With great skill he guides himself down the dangerous surface to where you sit in your fear. He takes you in his arms. You feel his warm, beating heart, and feel his breath on your face. Together, you traverse the cliff again and come to safety.

Once atop, he sets you on solid ground and sits down with you. You are ready to hear words like "Why did you wander off like that?" or "You foolish lamb!" You bow your head in shame. Instead he offers you complete forgiveness, and rejoices with you that you are safe. The past fades in your mind. No longer are you the naughty lamb who caused the shepherd great danger. No, that is gone. You are his, now, in this moment and forever, and he is yours. You lift your head and look full in his wonderful eyes. He tells you that he will never leave you orphaned. He tells you that the best gift ever given to Creation is his gift to you, and that this gift is the Holy Spirit, who is always as close as the next breath.

Then he commissions you to become the love and spirit of forgiveness that you have just encountered in him. He says, looking at you with great tenderness, "Peace be with you. And as the Father has sent me, so I send you." He breathes on you once again and says, "Receive the Holy Spirit. If you forgive the sins of any, they are forgiven them; if you retain the sins of any they are retained." And through his wonderful presence you ask the Holy Spirit to guide you in this path of forgiveness. You realize that you have been cleansed. A weight has been lifted from your shoulders. And you arise from the ground where you have been sitting feeling this lightness and freedom, and desiring to share it with everyone. Amen.

"MY SHEPHERD IS THE LIVING GOD" (v.1)
The New Century Hymnal

My shepherd is the living God,
I therefore nothing need;
In pastures fair, near pleasant streams
you settle me to feed.
You bring my wandering spirit back
when I forsake your ways,
And lead me for your mercy's sake
in paths of truth and grace.

Chapter 24

The Earth is Our Mother

Today, as we ponder the meaning of "Earth Day", let's think a bit about the "ways of knowing" that we value. For most people living after the 18th century, knowing came from a rather strictly outlined form of rationality. One was to trust the scientific method. One was to trust the tenets of philosophy. Where, I wonder, did some of the great minds of history come across their wisdom without these guidelines for thinking? As a mystic, I suggest to you today that much of pre-modern wisdom, at least found in the indigenous world, came from **intuition**, which some have called "conscious contact with God." This form of knowing arises from willingness on the part of people or tribes to be humble in the face of the Divine and **listen for guidance**. Our own Bible urges us not to lean on our own understandings. The wisdom of the 12 Steps of Alcoholics Anonymous urges us to surrender our lives and wills to God, and to seek through prayer and meditation to know God's will, and to pray for the power to carry it out.

Today, I'd like for us to consider and contrast the ways in which Americans have viewed and valued the earth. I had the privilege of studying the Native American spiritual leader known as Black Elk when I served a church in South Dakota. I came to see more clearly how the ways in which we think and the ways in which we value have a great impact on the actions we take in life. I'd like you to consider a paragraph from *Black Elk Speaks* by John G. Neihardt, who gathered stories from Black Elk before the great chief's death. The word "Wasichu" refers to people of European descent who colonized what we now call the United States.

> News came to us there in the Moon of the Falling Leaves (November) that the Black Hills had been sold to the Wasichus and also all the country west of the Hills—the country we were in then. I learned when I was older that our people did not want to do this. The Wasichus went to some of the chiefs alone and got them to put their marks on the treaty... Only crazy or very foolish men would sell their Mother Earth. Sometimes I think it might have been better if we had stayed together and made them kill us all.

Can you imagine "selling" your own mother? This is the regard that the tribes had for the Earth, that she is our mother. We have a long history of desecration of the Earth and its inhabitants. Hear these words from Black Elk:

> ...it was in the summer of my twentieth year (1883) that I performed the ceremony of the elk. That fall, they say, the last of the bison herds was slaughtered by the Wasichus. I can remember when the bison were so many that they could not be counted, but more and more Wasichus came to kill them until there were only heaps of bones scattered where they used to be. The Wasichus did not kill them to

eat; they killed them for the metal that makes them crazy (gold), and they took only the hides to sell... You can see that the men who did this were crazy. Sometimes they... just killed because they liked to do that. When we hunted bison, we killed only what we needed.

All our people now were settling down in square gray houses, scattered here and there across this hungry land, and around them the Wasichus had drawn a line to keep them in. The nation's hoop was broken, and there was no center any longer for the flowering tree. The people were in despair. They seemed heavy to me, heavy and dark; so dark that they could not be made to see any more.

I looked back on the past and recalled my people's old ways, but they were not living that way any more. They were traveling the black road, everybody for himself and with little rules of his own... I was in despair.

Black Elk's vision, as received in his childhood, was of a good red road of health, respect for self, others and creation. It was life within the sacred hoop. The black road, as alluded to above, was of a world filled with self-serving people who had lost their connection to the Great Spirit.

Perhaps the best story of our relationship to the Earth to be found in the Holy Bible in the first chapter of Genesis. It speaks of God's activities in creation. God looked upon creation and "God saw that it was good." God gave humans dominion over the earth. How do you think that we have done?

"PRAY FOR THE WILDERNESS" (v.1,5)
The New Century Hymnal

Pray for the wilderness, vanishing fast,
pray for the rainforest, open and vast.
Pray for the waterfalls, pray for the trees,
pray for the planet brought down by degrees.
Pray for the atmosphere, pray for the sea,
learn from the river, the rock and the tree;
Work til shalom in full harmony rings.
Trust the connection of all living things.

Chapter 25

The Keys to the Kingdom

There are some wonderful words spoken by Jesus to the disciples prior to his crucifixion. Sometimes the fourteenth chapter of John is called "The promise of the Holy Spirit." Jesus tells the disciples that he will be leaving them, but that he will not leave them orphaned. He shares that those who love him will keep his word, and that his Father will love them and with Jesus will make a home in their hearts.

Yes, Jesus knew that he was leaving. Many of the disciples were still in denial. He was, after all, their spiritual father, their leader, teacher and healer. They had not yet come into their own personal power, and Jesus needed to instruct them as to how this power would become their own. He shared that he would send another to instruct them. This will be the first time Jesus will use the word "Parakletos" to refer to the Holy Spirit. A parakletos is one who comes in to help the person who calls out to him for assistance in times of distress, doubt or bewilderment. Receive the Holy Spirit, who will always guide you. Let go of the rudder and call out.

I'd like to share a personal story that illustrates how the Spirit worked for me during a summer past. My congregation's rummage sale was to be held in our driveway, as neighbors were already planning a neighborhood sale and much of the advertising was already done. We had tons of "stuff." It was a challenge to mark and sell it. Not only that, but the weather turned threatening and some of the volunteers were plenty grumpy about the perceived lack of signage near our sale. I went to bed on Friday night weighed down with the burden of the perceived criticism and concerns about the weather.

Sometime during the night, I received a message that the following day I was to look for **only one thing**, and that was to be **any place whatsoever** where love was exchanged. You might say I was given a new pair of eyeglasses. I took this charge seriously and my mood lightened though the weather darkened. We laughed a lot, it rained a lot, and we ate sandwiches in the garage, where we had hauled as much rummage as it would store.

The following afternoon, I felt energized to put all of the damp, unsold clothes through the dryer to get them ready for the Vietnam Vets to pick up. Indeed as promised, God went before me to soften a heart and to overrule a resentment. I am so grateful for this experience.

As we ponder the "keys to the kingdom," we see that the role of the Holy Spirit is very important in this process. Calling upon the Spirit does require trust and an ability to relinquish control in our lives. In the book of John, Jesus reminds us of his commandments, which are different than the Ten Commandments. These are surprising to many, but the first is that we are to wash each other's feet. This means that we are to learn humility and practice servant leadership. The second of his commandments is that we are to love one another. And the third is this: "Do not let your hearts be troubled. Believe in God, believe also in me." This is a tough one for those of us who have a tendency to shelter troubled hearts. We are commanded not to do this. We are commanded to believe in God and believe in Jesus. People who have trouble believing in God and surrendering their lives and wills to God probably need a new God, one who desires to make all things possible in them, one who desires to be made manifest in them and make them shine.

One of the best books I've encountered on the teachings of Jesus is entitled *Love Without End: Jesus Speaks* by Glenda Green. In this segment, she speaks of the learning that can occur when we encounter bumps in the road, such as mentioned with the rummage sale story. She writes:

> Love is both a way of being and also a pathway for becoming. Love ignites life. Love savors life and sustains faith and hope. Even though life often brings lessons in hard packages, learning only happens when forgiveness has occurred and love is restored. It is love that ignites learning. Only with love can learning occur. That is how you take something from the school of hard knocks and transmute it into a permanent attainment. You can say, ' I don't have to do this again. I have completed the lesson. I know the meaning behind the experience.

She will go on to say, believing that Jesus has guided her to speak of it, "Love brings certainty to life, and when your love is clear and unpolluted with regrets or false desires, you will have the confidence to live your life with passion."

"SPIRIT OF THE LIVING GOD"

The New Century Hymnal

Spirit of the Living God, fall afresh on me.
Spirit of the Living God,
Fall afresh on me. Melt me, mold me, fill me, use me.
Spirit of the Living God, Fall afresh on me.

Chapter 26

Pentecost: The Outpouring of the Holy Spirit

It is Pentecost Sunday. Happy Birthday to the Christian church! Yes, today is our birthday and we are nearly 2000 years old! Let's talk a bit about the birthing of Christianity as a faith tradition, and then let's talk a bit about what is being birthed in our local church.

The events of the day of Pentecost are surprising yet expected. They are expected by many who read the gospel accounts. For instance, the Spirit is said to have co-created with Mary in order that she might birth Jesus. We know that the coming of the Spirit is promised by John the Baptizer when he states that one is coming who will baptize people in the Holy Spirit. The events of Pentecost are surprising and unexpected to the disciples, because they still cannot imagine themselves doing the work that Jesus did.

The book of Acts (referring to the acts of the apostles) gives us an amazing story of devout Jews from every nation who lived in Jerusalem. They were gathered, as was their tradition, seven weeks after Passover. According to the text, tongues of fire came to rest on each of the apostles and each was filled with the Holy Spirit and began to speak in other languages. The people gathered in the crowd were amazed. They wondered if the apostles were drunk!

They could not believe that they were hearing a multitude of languages being spoken by Galileans, who were notorious for being monolingual. If the disciples needed convincing that their mission was to have a scope beyond their group or nation, this surely provided it.

Peter, a fisherman, stands and speaks with authority about figures the crowd will recognize and trust. He speaks of Abraham, Moses, the prophets. And he lets the crowd know that the disciples are not drunk on new wine. They speak through the action of God as promised by Jesus. Thus begins a public ministry that will continue to be fueled by the Spirit's power. This ministry continues to be the heart and soul of the church today.

To me, the Holy Spirit, poured out on all on the day of Pentecost, is the greatest gift I have ever been given in my life. Why do I say this? Because to me, the Holy Spirit is *the agent of transformation*, the communication link between God and God's separated children. And I need transformation. I need to remember that all people are created in the image and likeness of God. I need to remember that we are all in this together. I need to remember not to judge, but to bless. I need to remember that when I'm growly and grumpy, I can always cry out to the Spirit, "Holy spirit, help me see this in a different way."

To me, the Holy Spirit, poured out on all on the day of Pentecost is a *great surpriser*. If this universe is just a ticking clock, wherein all can be understood by the mind and by mechanics, why should I bother to tick? But if this universe promises me new and fresh ways of understanding myself and others, not to mention limitless joy, I can't wait to get up in the morning to see what happens next!

To me, the Holy Spirit is a marvelous *house cleaner*. She helps me get the dust and grunge and cobwebs out of the deepest, darkest recesses of my psyche. She comes into the grubby basement of my soul with a flashlight, a bucket of fragrant soapy water and a sturdy mop. She throws open the heavy drapes and opens the windows. She helps me release my self-limiting thoughts and my desire to judge others as well as myself. When I start whining to her that I'm so weak or so useless, she looks me in the eye and says, "I am not listening to any of this." And she picks up her mop once more.

To me, the Holy Spirit is an *encourager and a comforter*. Jesus even referred to her as the comforter. She helps me to see that the times I am the most snarly are the times when some fearful, childish part of myself has become activated. She never stands there and yells "grow up!" She takes me onto her lap and rocks me and reminds me of who I am, the Beloved of God.

To me, the Holy Spirit is an *advocate*. Sometimes when I am so down or befuddled or so dismayed that I can't put one foot in front of the other, she intervenes for me, with sighs too deep for words. And God, who searches the heart, knows what is the mind of the Spirit, because the Spirit intercedes for me and for the saints according to the will of God. The Spirit helps me in my weakness.

To me, the Holy Spirit is *the great unifier*. All the little props my ego has manufactured to tell me I'm OK fall away in her presence, and so do everyone else's . All of a sudden it doesn't matter that I am white, or female, or educated, or a minister. All of a sudden it doesn't matter what you are, either, except that we realize who we are in God. And part of the reason we have church communities is to remind each other of that. I forgive you, you forgive me. Pretty soon all we are registering is the love that pours out when we forget to be afraid.

I ask you these questions: Has the Gospel been well-enough preached in this church for you to know that any church that preaches judgment has a hidden altar that does not serve God? Has the Gospel been well-enough preached that you know you were born to make manifest the love of God that is within you? Have you been assured that the Kingdom of God is within you and that you are capable of giving and receiving miracles? And has the Gospel been well-enough preached in this church for you to know that the Holy Spirit has always been creating, will create forevermore, and asks for only one thing, that you might receive her? If not, let me know, and I'll preach it again. I'll speak of it for as long as it takes to cast out the yoke of doubt. And we'll share it with all God's children. Amen.

"O HOLY SPIRIT, ROOT OF LIFE" (v.1)
The New Century Hymnal

O Holy Spirit, Root of life, Creator, cleanser of all things, anoint our wounds, awaken us with lustrous movement of your wings.

Chapter 27

Faith from the Inside

This message was penned in early June. I began it with a quote from Christopher Bamford, found in the Spring issue of *Parabola* magazine in 2001. "When we are at home in the garden, tending and nurturing all its plants, animals, and minerals, living with them through all the seasons and days, then healing comes upon us like a gift and makes us whole."

On some occasions, in the last church I served, we would abandon our usual worship setting and head for the cafe, where we could either write or share in small groups. That was the setting for this message.

A "family map" gives a person an opportunity to think back to early life experience. We might say that the early experience is a type of "seed bed" for beliefs that would form in our very beings. Sometimes when we review the beliefs that were instilled in us, we give thanks for them and continue to nurture them, like beautiful plants. Sometimes we come to see that certain beliefs are actually toxic to our spirits, and then we begin a process of dismantling them, of removing them as we would remove weeds from a garden.

It is important that we all consider the difference between religion and spirituality. Religion, to me, comes more from the head. It seems to be a series of prescribed beliefs, such as those found in creeds and doctrinal statements. Because I am a person who finds creeds to be divisive, I am grateful that this church does not emphasize them. Spirituality, on the other hand, seems to me to emanate more from the heart or soul of a person. In this regard, it is a very personal encounter with the Divine, rather than a set of teachings.

From my years as a family therapist, I have come to see that there are certain people in everyone's family tree or elsewhere in their early life (a neighbor, a teacher) who nurtured their spirit, and others who did not. I found it to be useful to ask people to reflect upon this question:

• **When you were a child, whose eyes lit up when you entered the room? Write about this person. How did they influence you?**

On the other side of the coin are those who adversely influenced our faith or spirituality, or perhaps our self concept:

• **Can you think of anyone whose presence harmed your young spirit? Write about this person. How did they influence you?**

Children's lives are lived in the presence of extended family, community, classmates and often a religious affiliation.

• **How important were faith, religious practice, and congregational life in your family? Has this changed in your adult life? How?**

For many people there comes a reexamination of faith issues at some point in adult life. It is easier for some to cut loose from experiences they now see as toxic. Others encounter much fear about being ostracized by their family, or being sentenced to hell by their religious leaders.

• **If you are a person who has re-visioned his/her faith, what obstacles did you have to overcome in the transfor-**

mation process?

It is not only people, but experiences that touch our very souls and help us feel more at home in the universe.

• **What experiences might you identify as those that bring you closer to God and to creation? Where, in this world, do you feel most deeply connected? Write about this place.**

Another clue to our soul messages is found in food and in ritual.

• **Are there certain foods that remind you of something important from your childhood? Which ones? When would you eat them? Who would prepare them? What feelings come to mind as you think of them?**

• **Were there certain rituals in your home or worship setting that were important to you, that fed your soul? What were they? What might they have meant to you?**

• **Are there rituals in your current worship or spiritual practice that you value? Are there some that might be missing?**

It is said that the ability to carry on in the face of adversity or suffering is cultivated in the realm of the soul or spirit.

• **Was there anyone in your childhood who demonstrated this ability? Write about this person. How have you yourself been able to hold onto your faith through difficult times?**

The word "Community" carries various meanings.

• **If you had a faith community to serve you now, what would it look like? If you could build an ideal faith community to serve you now, what would that look like?**

I encourage everyone who reads these words to answer

the questions and then find a trusted friend with whom to discuss all of this.

"God Made from One Blood"
The New Century Hymnal

God made from one blood all the families of earth,
The circles of nurture that raise us from birth,
Companions who join us to work through each stage
Of childhood and youth and adulthood and age.

Chapter 28

What Does Your God Desire?

What a pleasure it was to sit quietly in a corner of the Cafe last Sunday while the congregation sat at a number of tables and wrestled with various theological documents to try to articulate for ourselves just what we **believe.** Many who know us in our community are aware of what we **do** in terms of public service, but how many know what we **believe**, and how many of us can articulate that? Here is a synopsis of what the small groups came up with last week.

One table wrestled with the UCC Statement of Faith. They really wanted to know what it meant to be created in the image of God. Some of the concepts they gleaned were that God is inclusive, reconciling, forgiving, loving, non-judgmental and moves us beyond self-interest.

Another table, studying some statements made by Stephen Patterson in *The God of Jesus,* liked the statement that "The world can script your life if you let it." They spoke of how early conditioning teaches us the ways of "this world," but Jesus taught us of a transcendent reality known variously as "The Kingdom of God" or "The Reign of God."

One group wrestled with my Statement on Ministry and came away believing that inclusiveness is central to the message of the Gospel. A group working with the Eight Points of Progressive Christianity mentioned the importance of searching and questioning over the importance of "certainty." Folks at another table mentioned an important theme:

"How we behave is our testimony."

While I was sitting near the "Patterson Table," I over-heard how drawn some were to the statement that said, "This is what it means to call Jesus the Christ: It is to accept his vision of the banquet and the God who comes with it." Today's gospel lesson includes Matthew 9:9-13. It is a beautiful illustration of this banquet table theme. Jesus sits at a table with tax collectors and sinners. I think it is safe to say that the label of "sinner" was easily applied by all those who did not consider themselves to be one. Let us recall that the world in which Jesus' listeners lived was organized into a great hierarchy. At the top was the emperor, then his subordinates such as religious and military officials, local client kings, significant land holders and large-scale merchants. Below that one would find a small middle class of merchants and traders. But most of the people in the empire lived at a daily subsistence level. This group made up perhaps 80% of the population. These people were deemed unclean or expendable in their culture. As for the government, it sought to suck up as many of a province's resources as it could without provoking it into revolt or killing it off all together. In Patterson's words, "In Jesus we have come to know a God who renders impotent the power of dirt to keep the unclean outside the human community."

He goes on to say:

> In contrast to Rome's highly brokered empire, the Empire of God is that place where the means to life are offered freely. Jesus was an itinerant pundit,

who by his word and deed called into question the structures of his social world that dehumanized and made expendable so many human beings of God's own making. Indeed, he brought these expendables back into the human community. They were no longer unclean; he regarded them as clean. They were no longer ashamed; he treated them with honor. They were no longer sinners; he declared them righteous and able to stand in the glorious presence of God.

Jesus invites the disenfranchised to remember who they are. And he invites the powerful to give up their places in the web of a power-brokering culture and to become a beggar like him. This is what the eighth point of progressive Christianity refers to as "the renunciation of privilege." Privilege is yet another illusion from which we may free ourselves. For in God's Kingdom there is no dirt and no privilege. Amen

"O FOR A WORLD"
New Century Hymnal

O for a world where everyone
respects each other's ways,
Where love is lived and all is done
with justice and with praise.

Chapter 29

Healing Our Hopelessness

When I was growing up, our family loved to watch a TV show called "Gunsmoke." This cowboy western portrayed Marshall Dillon doing his durndest to bring law and order to the Wild West. There was a character on the show named Festus. He was a down-and-out sort of guy, as I recall. One day Marshall Dillon asked Festus how he was doing. Festus replied, "Well, Matt, I'm feeling kinda low. I feel lower than a snake's belly in a wagon wheel rut." That's pretty low.

In Jesus' time there was a man who was even lower than this. Jairus, a leader in the local synagogue, had a daughter who lay close to death. Those of us who have had children who became critically ill can identify with his panic and despair. When nothing seems to help our beloved child, we grow frantic. And if our child gets near to the point of death, we begin to feel helpless and hopeless and look everywhere for a solution.

Also in this story is an unnamed woman who had suffered with a hemorrhage for twelve years. According to Jewish law, she was unclean. She wasn't supposed to be in mixed company. She wasn't supposed to touch anyone. For twelve years she had lived as an outcast and spent all of her funds seeking a cure, none of which helped. She was helpless and hopeless.

Then, each of these two people heard about Jesus. And

for the first time there was a glimmer of hope. Some people call this story "the miracle on the way to a miracle." Jesus heard the despair in Jairus' voice and saw the hope and faith in his eyes. And so he began the walk to Jairus' house. On the way, he was interrupted. An unnamed woman ventured out in faith to touch his robe. We are told that Jesus experienced the power go forth from him, and he stopped to inquire as to what had happened. The woman came forth in fear and trembling and told the whole truth. The response of Jesus is the key to understanding his healing ministry: "Daughter, your faith has made you well; go in peace and be healed of your disease."

A minister named Billy Strayhorn tells us that he discovered that most real ministry, most life-changing ministry, takes place while doing other ministry. A miracle on the way to a miracle. These situations come when we are not prepared, when we're thinking about doing something else.

Ministry comes when we least expect it. The secret is keeping ourselves focused on Jesus and our relationship with God, so that we are able to discern those ministry moments, so that we are able to hear the call and prodding of the Holy Spirit.

As an illustration, Strayhorn tells of an acquaintance named Wayne, who is a Gideon. Wayne loves to share the Gospel. Well, Wayne started working for the Census Bureau. He was to gather statistics and not try to convert people. There was one man on his list that he was having a tough time locating. Finally, Wayne found him at home. This man had the "long form," which required a rather lengthy interview.

Wayne noticed as he filled out the answers that the man was on the brink of despair and was probably planning to take his own life. At the end of the interview, Wayne put his hand over his Census Bureau badge to cover it up and said to his sad interviewee, "Forget that I work for the Census Bureau for a minute. This is just me talking. You are God's property. Don't do what you are contemplating, it's wrong."

The next day, Wayne decided to check on this fellow. He called two or three times but could not reach him. So he decided to go by the man's home, but he was not there. As Wayne walked back to his car, the man strode up to him on the sidewalk and it was obvious that something had changed. He confessed to Wayne that his wife had left him and that he was contemplating suicide. He looked Wayne in the eyes and said, "Thank you. You saved my life." We never know when we might become a messenger of hope. Our only job is to extend the love of God when we can and when we are able. In Wayne's words, we are "God's Property." We were created to make manifest the love of God that is within us.

"LEAD US FROM DEATH TO LIFE" (refrain)
New Century Hymnal

Lead us from death to life, from falsehood to truth,
From despair to hope, from fear to trust.
Lead us from hate to love, from war to peace,
let peace fill our hearts, let peace fill our world,
Let peace fill our universe.

Chapter 30

"Can We Love Each One?"

It is a pleasure to spend some time together pondering another story from scripture where Jesus attempts to teach us about the Kingdom of God. This story is similar to one in which Mary anoints Jesus' feet with expensive oil. In that story, the extravagance of God's love is emphasized.

Today's story seems to turn more around themes of forgiveness, and the new life that springs forth in us when we genuinely feel forgiven.

Today's story contains a familiar point of contrast. We have a commoner and we have a Pharisee. The Pharisees believed that their salvation depended upon keeping God's law and staying apart from those who failed to maintain the same standards.

It seems rather unusual that a Pharisee would invite Jesus to dine in his home, for Jesus was not one of the accepted leaders of the day. The host, whose name was Simon, had apparently overlooked some of the welcoming behaviors that might have been extended to Jesus as the guest of honor. He does not offer water for foot washing, he does not extend a kiss of hospitality, nor does he anoint Jesus' head with oil. Simon will soon become upset by the chaos in his dining room for several reasons.

First of all, although it was not uncommon for regular folks to gather around the periphery of fine meals to catch a snatch of the teachings of the men gathered, it was highly unusual for a woman to make her way to the table. And it was highly unusual for a woman to let her hair down in the company of men, or to touch the men, let alone wipe their feet with tears, kiss their feet and anoint them. All of this she did for Jesus. These actions by the woman described as a "sinner" would be enough to cause the host great concern. Rules were being broken right and left. And the behavior of the woman shone a spotlight on Simon's own inattentiveness as a host.

But let's get past all of that to look at Simon's real deficiency. It is not his slighting of Jesus as a guest, but it is his spiritual pride. He works so hard to obey God's law that he no longer sees himself as a sinner. He sees a great gulf between himself and the woman in his house, but he fails to see the gulf between himself and God. If he perceived himself to be in need of God's grace, he cannot imagine that he would need much of it. The woman, on the other hand, is such a spiritual wreck that Simon cannot imagine her redemption. What can God do with such a person? Why would God bother? (These thoughts are from Dick Donovan)

Jesus grasps the situation as a "teachable moment." He tells a story of a creditor and two debtors. He is teaching Simon in a non-confrontive, roundabout way. In the story, a creditor has two debtors. One owes much, one owes less. The creditor forgives each of the debts. Jesus asks Simon, "Which of these will love him more?"

Simon grudgingly responds to Jesus' question that indeed, the one who owed more would be more grateful and would love the creditor more. Jesus, by announcing the woman's forgiveness, has performed a priestly function by restoring her to the community. Of course, only God was presumed capable of forgiving sins in that culture. So much he had to teach them, to teach us.

The title of this message indicates that I want us to think about each of these people, Simon and the woman, and try not to take sides. Simon was the product of a very patriarchal culture. He was a man of privilege. And by the rules of his day, he was successful and exemplary. The woman was not willing to live by the rules of Simon's day. She saw in Jesus a man who manifested a different type of regard for those around him. It was as though she needed to interact with him more and more until she could at last love herself with the love that he held for her and for all people. The Pharisee Simon was acting out the role that was scripted for him. Can we fault him for that? The love of Jesus pulled the woman out of her prescribed role as the village sinner and planted her feet firmly in the Kingdom of God. Jesus blessed her with this blessing: "Your faith has saved you. Go in peace."

I sometimes wonder if she was able to hold onto that faith in the culture in which she lived. I pray that it was so.

"An Outcast among Outcasts"
The New Century Hymnal

An outcast among outcasts, dismissed with double scorn,
belittled by the labels: "unclean" and "foreign born"—
came back with thanks for Jesus, and then went on away;
An outcast among outcasts showed grateful faith that day.

Chapter 31

Father's Day

Happy Father's Day! Today I would like to bring in a modern story of people playing their "cultural roles." This story is also strongly influenced by the concept of patriarchy, which might be shortened into the notion that "father knows best." Patriarchy makes certain presumptions about the role of women and the role of children, each of whom is to be subordinate to a man. Sometimes fathers can hang onto these presumptions well after their sons and daughters have reached adulthood.

Marriage and family therapist Frank Pittman tells us the story of such a man in his book *Man Enough: Fathers, Sons, and the Search for Masculinity.* Pittman, who is also a movie reviewer, calls upon the themes found in a 1970 movie for a segment of his book entitled "The Fatherless Father." The film is called "I Never Sang for My Father" and stars Melvyn Douglas as the father and Gene Hackman as his middle aged son. Each of these actors would be nominated for a best actor award that year. In the film, the two men confront each other on the day of the mother's funeral.

The son is staying with the father, helping him get ready for bed. They talk about the old man's life. The father was the son of a violent alcoholic, who ran out on his family. Then, as a boy, he had raised his younger siblings and had come through life feeling good about himself. Somewhat like Pharisee Simon, found in the previous sermon: A solid citizen, a good provider, a stable family man. He felt he was everything his father was not. Unfortunately, perhaps again like Simon, he offered no warmth, no vulnerability. He does not notice what his son senses so painfully: He has gotten no joy from raising his own children.

Throughout the course of the conversation, the younger man confesses to his father that he has never felt loved by him. He also shares his plan to marry a younger woman and move away from the area. "With sympathy, affection and great trepidation, the son invites the father to come live with them. The father refuses any help, announcing his credo and more: 'I don't need anybody. I can take care of myself. Who needs you? Out! I've lived my whole life so that I can look any man in the eye and tell him to go to hell!' Than night, the son left his father's house forever."

Pittman astutely points out that the father was completely blind to the notion that his restrained dignity and state of moral superiority were shields that he had adorned in his battle with his own father. And these shields would also keep his own son from getting close to him. We can perhaps feel pity for the alcoholic father who ran out on his family. And we can certainly feel pity for the son with the rock-hard father. But is there room in our hearts for the father in the middle, who girded his loins and took up his shield and became invulnerable? Is there not a touch of this overly-independent, intimacy-avoiding patriarch in all of us? Can we not admit that life seems simpler without emotions and wants and needs and negotiations?

Pittman concludes, "At the end, the son was thus left

unanointed by his father, unable to be the man in the re-lationship, the one who has the strength and the wisdom to protect and comfort the father. There was a healing that could not take place, and both father and son lived out the rest of their lives in loneliness."

I can't leave a sermon on such a sad note. Sports fans who read this paragraph will be able to put a date on it. It is about a story from national sports about a then-young bas-ketball player named LeBron James. He had become a "man of fire," scoring all but one point made by his team in the final overtime that led the Cavaliers to victory over the Pistons in the NBA. He had every right to be cocky and superior after his super-human efforts, but instead he spoke of his exhaus-tion and need for a good night's sleep. LeBron James was, at that time, the father of a toddler. Apparently he participated in the wake-up calls from this babe during the night. He told the reporters that he would be asking the child's grandmoth-ers if they might take care of the babe that night so LeBron could sleep off his exhaustion. This man makes enough mon-ey to buy a hotel to sleep in, but he wanted the best care for everyone. He wanted care for himself, for his wife and for their child. And he wasn't afraid to ask for help. Thank you, grandmothers everywhere, and thanks, LeBron James, for being a new man.

"WHEN LOVE IS FOUND" (v.3)
The New Century Hymnal

When love is tried and loved ones change,
hold still to hope, though all seems strange,
till ease returns and love grows wise,
through listening ears and opened eyes.

Chapter 32

Crossing the Unknown Sea

Today's Gospel lesson, about Jesus calming the stormy sea, imparts a beautiful understanding of the depth of the peace in Jesus' soul, a peace that could calm the frantic disciples, a peace that could calm the sea. This peace, of course, is the peace he wishes for each of us, especially at those times when our seemingly frail vessels are tossed about on wild and unpredictable waters.

The hymns that I selected for this message came from a section of our hymnal called "Comfort and Assurance." A verse of one of them is printed below. The hymn is variously called "My Life Flows on in Endless Song" and "How Can I Keep from Singing?"

The second verse of the hymn picks up the theme of the growing storm, which could potentially create great fear and discomfort. The phrase, "No storm can shake my inmost calm" means so much to me. This hymn reminds me that I am eternal, that I am of God, that although I have a body and an ego, I am neither. I am a creation and an emanation of the eternal. I will never die. I came from the light, and to the light I shall return. "No storm can shake my inmost calm." For me, this calm is cultivated daily in the spiritual practice of meditation, where all the insignificances of my life are left behind, where all the endless chatter of my fearful ego is silenced, where I sink below the surface of those choppy waters that are my sometimes life and observe them from the safety of the depths of my true identity.

The title of today's message comes from a book by David Whyte, who had a stormy passage in his life regarding the career he had chosen. My recollection of his work is that he had been some sort of corporate giant before electing to become a poet. The focus of his work now is to help corporate people understand that they need not shackle the poet in their souls, but can integrate it. He teaches people that "to have a firm persuasion in our work—to feel that what we do is right for ourselves and good for the world at the exact same time—is one of the great triumphs of human existence." His book is designed to "reawaken the sleeping captain in us before (our) soul crashes on the rocks."

Certainly the discernment of our vocation can involve crossing an unknown sea. But I would suggest to you today that there is another unknown sea that vexes and perplexes all people from time to time. That unknown sea is the contemplation of the death of our physical bodies. We can sometimes get caught in the web of predicting that the future is going to harm us in the same way be believe that past events have harmed us. There is a phrase for this: "Future Events Appearing Real." The first letters of each word spell "FEAR."

The very best way I know to keep fears from the past from influencing the future is to catch myself whenever I feel fear or pessimism and ask the Holy Spirit to give me a new interpretation. This is called "the holy moment." I used this approach when this sermon did not want to be born. I was stuck. I asked the Holy Spirit to help me. Soon I was busy doing some heavy-duty lawn and garden work. The next morning, some of the information I needed for this message was given to me, and the birthing of this message became easy instead of laborious.

It is a gift for me to be rereading this message as I type parts of it into a chapter of this book, *A Year of Hope*. Fear and dark thinking have been a part of my life for the past several weeks after I suffered a heart attack. I fell into a form of "post-traumatic stress" in which I was strongly averse to doctors, pills, and needles. But reviewing the calming of the sea by Jesus is helping me now. Thank you, Holy Spirit.

The Tibetan Book of Living and Dying tells us that those who are close to death are of course afraid. They see that they may be leaving everything they think they have ever known: their body, their home, their loved ones. Some people learn, very close to the time of their death, and some learn it earlier, that death is not the end. Those who learn it early give up their preoccupation with material things and find great meaning in simply extending love whenever possible.

I have sat with people who began communicating with the other side toward the end of their lives and they have taught me a great deal. For as John O'Donohue says in *Anam Cara*, "When a person is close to death, the veil between this world and the eternal world is very thin... Your friends who now live in the eternal world come to meet you, to bring you home."

"My Life Flows on in Endless Song" (v.4)
The New Century Hymnal

I lift my eyes; the cloud grows thin;
I see the blue above it;
And day by day this pathway smooths,
since first I learned to love it.
The peace of Christ makes fresh my heart,
a fountain ever springing;
All things are mine since I am Christ's--
how can I keep from singing?

Chapter 33

The Pursuit of Justice

As I type these words in 2018, I am aware of the many Americans who have demonstrated against the splitting up of would-be immigrant families along our border with Mexico. A plea has gone out from the protesters that anyone who speaks Spanish and who has concern for these families to come to Texas to help.

A message that I penned in 2007 carries some of these themes. Many people were weary of our country's war in Iraq and were demonstrating against it. One woman, named Cindy Sheehan, camped outside of then-President Bush's ranch to protest against this war. Her son Casey had been killed in Iraq.

Cindy became a figurehead for the anti-war movement, but after several weeks she said she just couldn't do it anymore. She said it was just too much for one person.

I had an opportunity to share her burden when a friend asked me to march with a peace group in our local rodeo parade. I was very busy getting ready for company, but a "still, small voice" told me to go and to help hand out the 1000 origami cranes that the peace group had made. Children adored them. I was glad I had awakened from my lethargy to march and to distribute them.

To my way of thinking, Cindy Sheehan's story was parallel to the story of the prophet Elijah. At one point in time, this great prophet just felt spent. He sat under a broom tree completely dispirited, tired, ready even to give up his life. His opponents were Jezebel and Ahab, who formed the government of his day. They were demanding that he quit serving God and begin serving Baal.

A message had come from Jezebel saying, essentially, "Tomorrow I will have you killed because you are the kind of minister who does not want to keep out of politics." Elijah fled for his life and sat under that broom tree. He said what Cindy Sheehan said, "I can't fight this battle anymore." For him, God had a different answer. Elijah was told that this was not the end of the road for him, that there was still work for him to do.

A man named Reverend Boesak, preaching in South Africa in 1998, in the height of apartheid, said it well. "God understands that there may come a time in the lives of people when we get tired. God understands that the struggle is long, drawn-out, painful, tearfilled, and that we may get tired. God understands that (so often) we have to get up and fight the same fight that you have been fighting for 10 or 20 or 50 years. You get tired. (But) as long as apartheid exists, we have work to do."

There was a government Minister in South Africa whom Boesak felt believed himself to be God. And Boesak answered, "Mr. Minister, you can threaten us all you like—Jesus Christ is Lord. You can come into the streets and into our churches and you can massacre us—Jesus Christ is Lord... No government can challenge the living God and survive. And that , Mr. Minister, is the good news for the people of God and the bad news for you!"

Eventually, in 1994, six years after Rev. Boesak preached his sermon, South Africa's first democratic, post-apartheid elections made Nelson Mandela president. Apartheid had been defeated.

In scripture, we are told that God requires three things of us: To love justice, to have mercy, and to walk humbly with our God. Indeed, social justice is one of the hallmarks of my denomination. It seems to me that the pursuit of justice is a long journey as we run into everything from stonewall opposition to lethargic apathy from others. The dictionary describes the word "just" as meaning "honorable and fair in one's dealings and actions, consistent with what is morally right, lawful, legitimate, suitable, fitting." The word justice refers to the quality of being just and fair, the principle of moral rightness and equity, the upholding of fair treatment and due reward in accordance with honor, standards or law. It isn't easy to love justice and to put that into action. Sometimes we just get tired and discouraged and want to go sit under a broom tree. Part of the reason we come together is to offer encouragement to each other in the pursuit of justice.

"GUIDE MY FEET" (v.1)
The New Century Hymnal

Guide my feet while I run this race,
guide my feet while I run this race.
Guide my feet while I run this race,
For I don't want to run this race in vain.

Chapter 34

Addressing God

As I reviewed my writing from past years on the Gospel of Matthew, I came across an interesting sermon illustration. In one sermon, I stated that bullying had become such an epidemic in our schools that federal agencies had stepped in to try to teach mediation skills to small children. Footage was shown of harsh aggression on the playground and in the lunch line. The response from the officials was to created a video for kindergarteners showing little pieces of chalk encountering bullying situations. The children were then encouraged to speak directly to the bully and try to resolve the problem. This was surprising but encouraging to me. I think my social training would have been to "tell the teacher." There are bullies on the playgrounds of the world, and there are bullies leading nations of the world. When bullies are not engaged successfully in human-to-human dialogue, people and nations can become very fearful. In the words of one of my friends, they seem to say, "My God or my military is mightier than yours. Let's rumble!"

We all desire safety and protection in this world, but the question is, "Who will provide it?" I was quite amazed by the progression of "God-Views" in today's various lectionary scripture passages. Let's look at them. Psalm 13 is a true psalm of lament. It is perhaps a child on the playground waiting for the teacher to come and smite his enemy. "How long must I bear pain in my soul, and have sorrow in my heart all day long? How long shall my enemy be exalted over me?"

In our second reading, Jeremiah 28:5-9, Jeremiah acknowledges all of the prophets who have gone ahead of him who seem to speak for a punishing God. "The prophets who preceded you and me from ancient times prophesied war, famine, and pestilence against many countries and great kingdoms." Can you see the same God-concept as the Psalmist presented? God the punisher, God holding all power. But now listen to Jeremiah's last phrase: "As for the prophet who prophesies peace, when the world of that prophet comes true, then it will be known that the Lord has truly sent that prophet."

What I think is happening here is that Jeremiah is prophesying that we will grow up from the stance of the Psalmist (imploring God for intervention) to people who more closely resemble the disciples whom Jesus is sending forth in Matthew.

Today's very short Gospel lesson (Matthew 10:40-42) requires a bit of research into the context of Jesus' teaching. Previously in this chapter, Jesus has summoned the disciples and given them healing powers and authority over unclean spirits. He gives them marching orders. He warns that they will face persecution. He tells them not to fear the person who can kill the body. He assures them of God's love. He asks that his word be acknowledged among people. He warns that he has come with a sword.

In my opinion, the gist of today's Gospel lesson is Jesus saying to the disciples, "Become my message." This is a far cry from "O God, rescue me." Jesus is asking us, the modern day disciples, to grow up. In the words of one sermon writer, God initiated a four-way partnership. God sent Jesus, Jesus sent the disciples, the disciples go, and those who welcomed the disciples take the final step by providing support.

During my midlife years, my dear father, the son of a minister, said he would give me his blessing to enter the ministry if I promised not to let the ministry break my spirit. Part of that effort, for me, is to move beyond the child on the playground calling out for the teacher. This is one aspect of God—protection—but not the only one. When I asked God to help me with my feelings of being overwhelmed by the needs of the world, I was instructed to forgive myself for not being able to answer the world's every need. I was instructed to forgive all who fall short. It was made known to me that guilt is a heavy burden. I was reminded of a statement by the modern theologian Frederick Buechner that "the place God calls you is the place where your greatest joy meets the world's deepest need." I was reminded that Jesus said, "My yoke is easy and my burden is light."

We are partners with God, receiving the prophets and welcoming the holy, those who cause us to stand a little straighter. We are here to offer a cool drink of living water to those who thirst for Spirit and not condemnation. Thanks be to God.

"Called as Partners in Christ's Service" (v.2)

The New Century Hymnal

Christ's example, Christ's inspiring,
Christ's clear call to work and worth,
let us follow, never faltering,
reconciling folk on earth.
Men and women, richer, poorer,
all God's people, young and old,
blending human skills together,
gracious gifts from God unfold.

Chapter 35

On the Trail to Miracles

Some wonderful things happened one summer week in 2011. I was grateful to have eyes to see them. Sometimes when apparent crises of one type or another try to pull our eyes to one issue only, we miss the small miracles that go on all around us, all the time.

The first miracle I recall happened at the church rummage sale. It was about 2:30 on that Saturday afternoon. We were beginning to box up some items that had not been sold. We had decided to lower to half price all of the remaining rummage. A couple approached our tables. They looked over a set of cookware. I'm thinking it was marked $10.00. We tried to explain that everything was now half price. The man fished in his pocket and pulled out $4.00. They looked sad. We said that $4.00 was plenty for all of the cookware. Karen began to explain this in Spanish. Their faces glowed in gratitude. It was not they who received the greatest gift in that transaction. It was we who saw the currency of love being exchanged.

A second miracle happened on Sunday when a woman I'd met at Life Care Center showed up as a guest of one of our musicians. Mary was facing one of life's most difficult transitions, that of giving up house and home and settling into assisted living, but she still sang praises to God. What a beacon of hope it is to see faith outliving fear. Mary, like Joe, faced issues of mobility. My heart breaks when I think of all the older folks who can't get out to enjoy the incomparable beauty of nature in June here in the mountains. I'm grateful for all who bring them out of their "facilities" to do so.

Still another miracle visited me when I sent out an email requesting to hear about other memories of past rummage sales or of Bluegrass worship. Much to my surprise, some previous members who have moved away but still ask to stay on our email list answered right away. Jillann wrote from Burundi to remember a past rummage sale in which folks came together to help, laugh, socialize with the buyers, and have a lovely day. She said it felt very communal to her.

Markie wrote to say that she remembered a Bluegrass Sunday when Keith climbed into our treehouse with her son Jack and both looked out. She feels that Keith was older than 80 at the time, and that she would never forget that wonderful grin on his face.

Juanita responded to my request by sharing a memory from the most recent sale. Ken and Bud did a quick overhaul on two fishing rods and reels, making them receiver-ready for a single mom and her son so they could fish together.

That Wednesday, a *Denver Post* story of this ilk was printed. It seems that a Denver commercial real estate broker named Joe Carabello had driven past Sonny Lawson Park at 24th Street and Welton Street downtown. The memories flooded in. It was the ball field was where he had played baseball as a kid. His father, who taught him, had played and coached and later umpired there as well.

Yet on that sun-drenched afternoon, the field lay empty while around its edges several dozen obviously homeless men and women rested in the shade of the surrounding trees.

Alas, dear reader, my sermon notes simply state "Tell the Story." That was seven years ago. But I seem to recall that Mr. Carabello took it upon himself to organize ball games on that site, and that a nearby Subway shop even provided sandwiches.

Giving and Receiving: Who receives the greatest blessing? We sold some pots and pans at a good price to some immigrants at our rummage sale. They were so grateful. A man offered a ride to a mobility-impaired woman so she could hear him play Bluegrass music at our outdoor service. But who received the greatest blessing when we heard this woman proclaim her faith in God? A mom and her son went fishing together, but whose hearts were most filled with the joy of giving? A man reached into his soul out of the love of baseball and those who taught it to him. He provided an opportunity to pay that love forward. Another man wrote it up for the newspaper so we could all share in that love-filled impulse that moves us beyond self-interest.

Thanks be to God!

"FOR THE FRUIT OF ALL CREATION" (v. 4)
The New Century Hymnal

For the harvests of the Spirit, thanks be to God.
For the good we all inherit, thanks be to God.
For the wonders that astound us,
for the truths that still confound us,
Most of all that love has found us, thanks be to God.

Chapter 36

"Movin' On"

In Chapter 9 of Luke, Jesus had called the disciples together and gave them power and authority over all demons
and the ability to cure diseases. He sent them "to preach
the Kingdom of God and to heal the sick." What wondrous
works they would do! He also told them to travel light, no
purse for money, and to rely on the hospitality of local folks
for food and housing. It was his way of saying, "Trust God
to provide."

Yet Jesus was no starry-eyed optimist. He knew that
there would be those who would not receive the disciples.
So he taught them how to deal with rejection. He said, "As
many as don't receive you, when you depart from that city,
shake off even the dust from your feet for a testimony against
them." It was a way of "movin' on," of not wasting time and
effort on those who did not wish to receive the spiritual gifts
that the disciples had to offer.

Jesus taught them this method of dealing with rejection
and we see how he, himself, employed it. You see, he had to travel through Samaria to get to Jerusalem, and there were a lot of
folks in that region who wanted nothing to do with his teachings. Jews and Samaritans didn't have much to do with each
other. We are told that the Samaritans "didn't receive (Jesus),
because he was traveling with his face set toward Jerusalem."

Let me ask you this question: If you knew that you only
had a few weeks to live, would you continue to put up with

bad behavior from other people? Would you be inclined to engage in chit-chat and small agendas? What the scripture lesson is telling us is that by "setting his face toward Jerusalem," Jesus was pondering the end of his bodily life on this planet. So, when the Samaritans refused to impart hospitality, he elected to "move on." But this did not sit well with his two hot-headed disciples, James and John, the "Sons of Thunder." No, they wanted revenge. Recalling the story of Elijah from their Jewish history, they implored Jesus to let them call down fire from heaven to incinerate those inhospitable Samaritans! But Jesus rebuked them saying, "The Son of Man did not come to destroy ...lives, but to save them." There would be no revenge agendas for Jesus.

Jesus then told these "Sons of Thunder" that they were too focused on the **privileges** of discipleship and what they could GET or DO, and that they must look at the **responsibilities** of discipleship, meaning what they could GIVE.

I once came across a charming story written by a woman pastor. She wrote of living abroad after graduating from college. The first six months, she was "awash in loneliness." She'd buy a paperback novel each afternoon and fill her evening with that. She'd meet with a clump of other teachers each weekend and they would bash the culture in which they were living. Her homesickness increased. She eventually decided to try to engage the country on its own terms. She stayed in town one weekend and went to a church near her workplace.

The second time she showed up, the usher remembered her, and his kindness brought tears to her eyes. The third time, she did not duck out after the final hymn but stayed for fellowship. She wrote, "The effect of that loving, laughing, singing congregation's connection to Jesus Christ would come to permeate every aspect of my life. It was a wondrous thing to stumble into the hands of the living God." (Holtz-Martin, *Feasting on the Word*)

Jesus didn't want to sell discipleship under false pretenses. He wanted people to know what they were getting into. He wanted them to know up front that being his disciple would be demanding: A tough row to hoe. He dismissed easy discipleship by saying that people could and would be homeless. He dismissed a plea to bury a father and another to go say goodbye to family. He said, "No one, having put his hand to the plow, and looking back, is fit for the Kingdom of God." He saw that **forward movement** was essential for discipleship.

I think that the woman who lived in a foreign country and who resisted that country lived as the disciples first did, with an element of defeat ("why can't these people be more like me?"). But she moved to a state of acceptance. "Finally it was make-or-break time. I would cut the ties that bound me to my discontent and try my host country on its own terms." Amen.

"GOD, SPEAK TO ME, THAT I MAY SPEAK" (v.1)
The New Century Hymnal

God, speak to me, that I may speak
in living echoes of your tone; as you have sought,
so let me seek your erring children lost and lone.

Chapter 37

Abundance

The dictionary defines greed as "an excessive desire for more than one needs or deserves." The attitude of needing **more** is cultivated in us from an early age. Even cartoon stations have advertisements. Sunday newspapers seem to be about half advertising. The evening news is loaded with stories and ads for prescription meds, generally aimed at gray-haired consumers. The underlying message is this: "You are not sufficient. Unless you have the vigor and attractiveness of the folks in this ad, you are missing out. You need this pill or this car or these home furnishings in order to be adequate, secure, fulfilled." Wow. That is a bitter **pill** to swallow! But it is craftily presented to play on our insecurity, and thus produce sales.

There was no glossy advertising in Jesus' day, but there was plenty of insecurity, for it is a part of the human condition. We are presented, in Luke 12, with a man who is anxious and insecure about his financial status. As Jesus is teaching, a man in the crowd who feels that his brother has not given him his just inheritance calls out to Jesus to act as a judge in the case. Jesus responds by teaching that the quality of one's life is not measured in possessions, but in one's openness to hearing and doing the will of God. He then goes on to illustrate the point with a parable about a farmer with an abundant crop and what he chooses to do with it. He builds larger barns to store and **hoard** his "bumper crop."

We learn several things about this farmer. First, he does not seem to hold himself accountable to or responsible for anyone else. Maybe he is a rugged individualist. His gain is **his** gain, and no one else shall prosper from it. Perhaps he sees himself as needing no one else, so why help others? They should strive to reach the same self-sufficiency that he has reached! We come to surmise that another feature of this man is that he does not need others nor does he seem to hear, need or heed God. The farmer does not recognize God as the source of abundance, nor is he willing to act as a faithful steward of God's abundance.

How antithetical it is to come to realize that "too much" is actually bad for us. Why? Because it represents clutter, excess, reliance on material goods, and a mass of **things** that we now have to store, insure and protect. When "give us this day our daily bread" is translated from the Aramaic, it becomes "give us this day what we need in bread and insight." How different this story would be if the farmer had recognized God as the source of blessing. Not only would his life have been secure, but also the lives of those for whom he would become the conduit of God's provision.

In her remarkable book, *The Artist's Way*, Julia Cameron gives modern people some very fine food for thought regarding our perceptions of God. Listen to her words as she tells a story of a woman named "Nancy."

"I'm a believer," Nancy declares. "I just don't believe God gets involved with money." Although she doesn't recognize it, Nancy carries two self-sabotaging beliefs. She believes not only that God is Good—too good to do money—but also that money is bad. Nancy, like many of us, needs to overhaul her God concept in order to fully recover her creativity.

For most of us, raised to believe that money is the real source of security, a dependence on God feels foolhardy, suicidal, even laughable. When we consider the lilies of the field, we think they are quaint, too out of it for the modern world. We think that **we** are the ones who will keep clothes on our backs. **We** are the ones who buy the groceries. And **we** will pursue our creativity, we tell ourselves, when we have enough money to do it easily. And when will that be?

During my first summer in Evergreen, I went to Walmart to purchase school supplies for children in need. I was lost. I blurted out to a nearby young mother, "Excuse me, is that the Evergreen school list you are carrying?" She brought her list over to me and told me where to find the school supplies. She mentioned what she thought would be wise choices, and what to steer away from. This woman did not have to do any of this. She could have said to herself, "I don't have the time or energy to deal with this uninformed woman," and walked away from me.

She was quite different from the farmer in today's scripture lesson. She extended herself to help another. I have come to see that stinginess is a weed that must be pulled from the garden of our souls. And stinginess isn't just about money. It's about all the gifts we have: time, willingness to help, joy, support, and encouragement.

"DEAR GOD, EMBRACING HUMANKIND" (v.1)
The New Century Hymnal

Dear God, embracing humankind,
forgive our foolish ways;
Reclothe us in our rightful mind,
in purer lives your service find,
in deeper reverence, praise.

Chapter 38

Let Your Light Shine

This message comes from Mark 6:1-13, and in my notes I see that credit was due to Beverly Zink-Sawyer of Union Seminary in Virginia. I thank her for letting **her** light shine.

In this scripture lesson we see Jesus being mocked by his hometown folks when he preaches in the synagogue. What did he do to earn this disrespect? What is it about "familiarity that breeds contempt," as the old saying goes? Jesus' rejection in his hometown of Nazareth proves the old adage to be true. Familiarity breeds contempt. After performing miracles on both shores—and in the middle—of the Sea of Galilee, he returns to the town where he has grown up and lived an ordinary early life. He goes to the place where any Jewish teacher would go: To the synagogue, where he teaches the hometown crowd. Perhaps it is the unexpectedness of the event that precipitated the reaction of the people—the fact that the townsfolk are not expecting to see "little Jesus," who grew up around the corner, or "Jesus the carpenter," who had fashioned their tables and benches, in the role of wise prophet of God. Obviously his teaching astounds them but also strikes a nerve.

At first they are captivated. "Where did this man get all of this?" they ask. "What is this wisdom that has been given to him? What deeds of power are being done by his hands!" In other words, they reason, it is still the Jesus we have always known—and we know he is just one of us, not any miracle worker, they must say.

What prompts such a negative, outrageous response to Jesus from the neighbors in Nazareth? Exploring the reasons for the human emotions revealed in this text gives us a clue as to why Mark includes it in his Gospel. Surely it is not a flattering portrait of the community in Nazareth or of Jesus himself. The people come across as mean-spirited and mocking. And Jesus responds that prophets are not received in their own hometowns.

How would **we** have reacted, had we been in the position of the characters portrayed? What would we think about a neighbor whom we believed to be just an ordinary, hardworking man turning into a miraculous teacher, let alone the reputed Son of God? I venture to guess that we all would have our share of skepticism. After all, we tend to see what we expect to see and are slow to accept challenges to our preconceived assumptions. There is an example of this from my own memory bank that I think I will always share whenever this story comes up for consideration.

When our son was in high school, he played basketball. One of the arch rivals of his school, Brandon Valley, was Mitchell High. After Tony had left to go to college, my husband and I went to the state basketball championships in Rapid City just for old time's sake. Mitchell, a perennial powerhouse in basketball, had made it to the finals. If memory serves me, they had defeated Brandon to get there. But here is the crucial point: There was an absolutely outstanding young man playing on the team from Mitchell. And the Brandon folks would not accept this. They labeled him as cocky, as "full of himself." They demonized him and made catcalls during the final game. I was astounded at this response. I even had my husband stop in Mitchell on our way home so I could apologize to the people there for the behavior of some of the Brandon folks against this player. Perhaps you have heard of him. His name is Mike Miller and he was later a member of the 2012 NBA championship team, the Miami Heat.

Do we really believe that God can do great things, or that we can? We seem to be shaped by those around us, not by our faith. My friend Lila, who taught at the University of South Dakota, told me about a phenomenon in the Native American culture known as "the crab barrel phenomenon." We were walking in a city park one evening and she pointed out a group of Native American students. She said they were among the few that could find their way off the reservation. She said that when a young person attempts to go to college or better themselves, they are like a crab trying to climb out of the crab barrel. Instead of cheering them on, the other crabs will reach up and pull that crab with aspirations back into the crowd. How many young Native Americans have become small in order to avoid this dilemma?

I'd like to close with a wonderful quote from Marianne Williamson in her book *A Return to Love*. It is sometimes attributed to Nelson Mandela, but was penned by Williamson:

> Our deepest fear is not that we are inadequate. Our deepest fear is that we are powerful beyond measure. It is our light, not our darkness, that most fright-

ens us. We ask ourselves, 'Who am I to be brilliant, gorgeous, talented and fabulous?' Actually, who are you not to be?"

You are a child of God. Your 'playing small' does not suit the world. There is nothing enlightened about shrinking so that other people don't feel insecure around you. We were born to make manifest the glory of God that is within us. It is not just in some of us. It is in everyone.

 As you let your light shine, you unconsciously give other people permission to do the same. As you are liberated from your own fears, your presence automatically liberates others.

Amen.

"THIS LITTLE LIGHT OF MINE"
New Century Hymnal

This little light of mine, I'm gonna let it shine.
This little light of mine, I'm gonna let it shine.
This little light of mine, I'm gonna let it shine...
let it shine, let it shine, let in shine!

Chapter 39

Physical and Spiritual Healing

Children and adults alike will hear today about the amount of practice it takes to gain proficiency in music. The point I want to make today is that this amount of practice is also required to achieve peace of mind.

Today, in addition to telling you that I spent many, many hours as a child practicing my flute, I also want to tell you how musicians help other musicians. Or how Christians can help other people, or how Jewish prophets can heal Gentiles. It's all part of the milk of human kindness.

Here's a little story for you: One of the great aspects of computer memory is that I can save my sermons and see how I or we or the world has evolved in three-year increments. In the spring of 2007, Elsa, our choir director, was encouraging me to play my flute with the choir in May. I looked at the piece. Five flats! I didn't even know what the fifth flat was! I felt much anguish about this situation, the flames of the fire being fanned by knowledge that I needed to give many hours to a grant application. This would curtail flute practice time.

I prayed that I might receive discernment in this matter, and the answer came in the form of a message from a daily meditation book. A Danish proverb was quoted. "Better to deny at once than promise long." The text went on to say that those of us who struggle with the ability to say "no" to others can be very problematic for others because we keep them dangling and coming back to find out whether we mean "yes" or "no" or yet another "we'll see." I saw myself in this story.

The writer went on to say, "Fear is at the root of my inability to refuse. Someone may get angry or be displeased or write me off. But I cannot be responsible for the way people react to the choices I make... all I can do today is try to carry out God's will for me as I see it. If I'm wrong, I will stand corrected and make my amends. I believe that, too, is God's will." This prayer was found at the end of the meditation: "God, grant me the courage to be honest and say No if that is what I mean." I did decline to play and I quit leaving the music folks dangling.

And so the spiritual task for me was to deal with indecisiveness. I was being invited to participate in my own **spiritual** healing, just as Naaman was invited to participate in his **physical** healing when Elisha told him how to heal his leprosy. (2 Kings 5:1-14)

In the interim between 2007 and 2010, a miracle happened. Elsa asked me once again to play the flute descant with 5 flats, and our lovely pianist Jeri volunteered to put the whole piece in the key of C for me (no sharps or flats). I played it with joy. This is how we help each other. Soon, we will figure out how to fight compassion fatigue for those who serve our churches as leaders. Together, we make things better. Amen

"O Christ, the Healer, We Have Come" (v. 1)

The New Century Hymnal

O Christ, the healer, we have come
to pray for health, to plead for friends.
How can we fail to be restored
when reached by love that never ends?

Chapter 40

Who is My Neighbor?

Ayoung lawyer tried to justify himself by asking Jesus a question. Jesus had just taught about how we are to love our neighbor as ourselves, and the young man wanted to know, "And who is my neighbor?" Jesus told a story that many of us learned as children.

Two religious leaders, a priest and a Levite, were walking toward Jericho. Each saw a man laying beaten at the side of the road but avoided the situation. The person who carried the wounded man to safety was a Samaritan: He was of a group despised by the Jews. Then Jesus asked his questioner, "Who proved to be the neighbor to the man who was beaten?" The young man answered, "The one who showed mercy on him." Jesus replied, "Go and do likewise."

Several millennia later, in 2004, a woman sits at a word processor reflecting on the story of the Good Samaritan. She expands the lens of her mind to see Jesus telling the story to a lawyer, whose training is in Torah or sacred law. The lawyer wants a checklist, so he can make sure he inherits eternal life. He decides to joust a bit with the young rabbi Jesus.

The woman's mind and heart comprehend the classism and legalism inherent in the setting. There is a certain smugness amongst the people who have made it their life's work to know and follow numerous religious laws. You might say they were **card-carrying religious elite** people. They were men, they were educated, they relied on their minds, they did everything they could to obey the Torah.

The woman's mind sits with the arrogance she perceives. It seems so similar to the arrogance that nations can build. The pride of the student of the Torah at the expense of the Samaritan people seems so very much like the pride of the American people at "crushing" anyone who purportedly stands in our way.

The lawyer asks a tough question. "And who is my neighbor?" On the surface, the lawyer is asking who he must love. But he also wants to know who he is **not** required to love.

How was the Samaritan able to love a beaten man at the side of the road? He probably could not even identify the man to ascertain his nationality or social class. The woman thought about the man beaten at the side of the road.

She saw this man every night on the 5:30 news. He was a dead man in Iraq or a wailing mother in Palestine or a starving child in the Sudan. She saw him every day in the *Denver Post*. He was a drug dealer who was knifed in Denver, or a person with no health insurance and a $63,000 hospital bill. Her heart ached for these people. And she felt so paralyzed and overwhelmed that like the priest and the Levite, she crossed over to the other side of the road. She turned off the television and put down the newspaper.

Like the lawyer, she longed for a recipe to help her out of confusion or despair. She prayed and received the same answer that the lawyer had received from Jesus. That she was to outgrow her need for a superhero leader or a superhero God who would crush the enemy. She was called instead to a God of Mercy whose reign or "neighborhood" encompassed all of creation. She was to lovingly set aside her long-cherished goals of safety, comfort, and the esteem of others. She was to continue to speak of difficult topics in the name of justice, mercy and humility. Amen.

"They Asked, 'Who's My Neighbor?'"
The New Century Hymnal

They asked "Who's my neighbor and whom should I love;
for whom should I do a good deed?"
Then Jesus related a story and said,
"It's anyone who has a need, yes, anyone who has a need."

Chapter 41

Mrs. Jones, the Teacher

There is a passage in Luke 12 that makes me think of an elementary school teacher. The passage is about a master who leaves his estate but comes back to find his household in good order, thanks to his responsible servants.

I imagined an elementary school teacher, whom I called Mrs. Jones, who was needing to leave her classroom for a very short time, perhaps to run an errand to the principal's office. The class immediately falls into wild chaos. They post a sentry at the door to warn of the teacher's return.

Spit wads fly. Goofy words are scribbled on the chalkboard. Chaos reigns. Then the sentry shouts out "She's coming!" And spit wads are hidden and goofy words erased. By the time the teacher returns, a group of little angels with sweet smiles on their faces sit upright in their desks, all the while knowing they've enjoyed their moments of chaos quite a bit.

Little children have so much energy! My hat goes off to every teacher who has the dubious pleasure of trying to keep enough order in the room to ensure that those who want to learn have the opportunity to do so! Some of the children will see the teacher as their ally in the classroom. Others, for whatever reason, will see their teacher as an opponent, or someone who wants to keep them down.

Similarly, some adults will see God as a source of assurance, a port in the storms of life. Others will see God as a harsh judge. Let's not forget your parents. How do they fit into the equation? Were they loving and encouraging, or were they belt-strap wielding disciplinarians? Perhaps you had one of each. Theologian Matthew Fox tells us in his book *A New Reformation* that fundamentalism, which portrays God as a punishing father, is a religion based on control and dominant and domineering patriarchy. Meister Eckhart, a mystic from the distant past, tells us that "All the names we give to God come from an understanding of ourselves." Thus, people who worship a punishing father are themselves punishing people.

What does this have to do with school children? If you still carry around fear of authority from your school days, you may still be carrying around fear of a punishing God. Fox tells us that unhealthy religion and spirituality come from fear of chaos, fear of the feminine, and fear of trust!

Now let's go back to our metaphor of the elementary school classroom. Mrs. Jones has returned from the principal's office. Instead of finding smirking and quasi-obedient students in their desks, she finds relaxed kids chatting among themselves. Oh, there are troublemakers, but their peers have reached out to them and asked them to please run their energy off at recess, because there are some very neat things they can learn from Mrs. Jones if they can all calm down and put their heads together.

Mrs. Jones does not stress competition. There is no shame in her classroom. Students are taught to takes turns talking. They learn to show respect for the contributions of others. They learn to keep their comments focused on the material they are studying. They value cooperation and the uncovering of new ways of being together.

Once we realize that there is nothing to fear and that we were placed into this earthly realm to enact peace and to promote harmony, we can relax. We don't have to do great things or find our photo on the front page of the local newspaper. We just get to wake up every morning and go about our business, wondering in a happy way when the next chance will come to offer someone a hand up, or to enjoy the beauty of the universe, or discover a way to do something that had always seemed difficult. Our lives become a beautiful banquet.

"There's a Spirit in the Air"
The New Century Hymnal

There's a spirit in the air,
telling Christians everywhere:
"Praise the love that Christ revealed,
living, working in our world."

Chapter 42

A Clenched Fist

Many years ago, when I penned this message, I recall that the readings were at once beautiful and challenging. Jesus had given the gathered people lessons about not hoarding their wealth or their compassion. He challenged them, and us, with these words: "Fear not, little flock, for it is your Father's good pleasure to give you the kingdom." And he teaches them, and us, that where our treasure is, there will our hearts be also. We are to lay up treasures in heaven, not hoard earthly possessions or our compassion.

As I wrote from these scriptures, I had an image in my mind of a clenched fist. Not necessarily a fist clenched in anger, but one grasping hard onto what is known. Henri Nouwen tells a story in his book *With Open Hands* about an elderly woman who is taken into a psychiatric ward. She is clutching something fiercely in her hand. Several orderlies must use their full strength to remove it. It turns out to be an old coin. Her fear was that if she let go of that last possession, she would have nothing more and be nothing more.

I believe that at some deep level, Jesus is asking us to let go of the last coin in order to see that we will not cease to be, that we will not disintegrate. Instead, we will see that we are much more than what we own or what level of education we have attained, or the degree of health we possess. We just might see that we are conduits for the power of God, that within us is the capability to bring the Reign of God right into this world today. Every time we share our joy and abundance, every time we feel our feelings rather than act them out on some other person, every time we reconcile instead of going off mad, we are bringing the Kingdom close.

I found a wonderful statement from Pema Chodron, a Buddhist teacher. I think it fits beautifully into this notion of seeing beyond "our stuff." Here is what she says:

> I think that all of us are like eagles who have forgotten that we know how to fly. The teachings are reminding us who we are and what we can do. They help us notice that we're in a nest with a lot of old food and old diaries, excrement and stale air. From when we were very young we've had this longing to see those mountains in the distance and experience that big sky and the vast ocean, but somehow we got trapped in that nest, just because we forgot we knew how to fly. We are like eagles, but we have on underwear and pants and shirts and socks and shoes and a hat and coat and boots and mittens and a Walkman and dark glasses, and it occurs to us that we could experience that vast sky, but we'd better start taking off some of this stuff. So we take off the coat and the hat and it's cold, but we know that we have to do it, and we teeter on the edge of the nest and we take off. Then we find out for ourselves that everything has to go. You just can't fly when you are wearing socks and shoes and coats and underwear. Everything has to go.

Chodron's book *Start Where You Are: A Guide to Compassionate Living* teaches us very specifically how to retrain our thoughts in order to guide us into more openness with others. For instance, when a person who annoys us comes into the scene, we can put up our walls or seek distance or begin the tapes about what a jerk this person is. Or we can sit with our feelings and perhaps discover that the very thing that drives us nuts about this person is some attribute we can't forgive in ourselves. So we sit with our harshness and we forgive ourselves for our vulnerabilities and then this person becomes less annoying. All of this is part of spiritual practice. It helps us to unclench our fists, if you will.

I believe that parables of Jesus are designed to help us unclench our fists as well. We hold tightly onto our stuff, and Jesus softly asks us to share it. He promises that there is a kingdom that we will come to know when we can unclench our fists and become compassionate, as he indeed is compassionate. My dear friends, I want to tell you that this fist unclenching is no easy thing. We'd better not try to do it in our last few hours of life. The kingdom of God is within us, waiting to be born, waiting to soar like that eagle.

"On Eagle's Wings" (v. 1)
Chalice Hymnal

You who dwell in the shelter of the Lord,
who abide in God's shadow for life,
say to the Lord:
"My refuge, my rock in whom I trust."

Chapter 43

A Short Chapter
for Our Children

It was a custom, in all the churches I served, to make the last Sunday before the public school classes began a time to focus on our kids and what lay ahead of them both in school and in life. It behooves us, we adults, to look back and see how many of these prayers came true in our own lives. It is never too late to learn.

The Blessing of the Backpacks: We sense that the protection of children is a very old theme in our Judeo-Christian story. We recall with pleasure the story of the crafty midwives who saved the baby Moses from Pharoah and packed the babe off in a tiny cradle boat woven of reeds. We remember the story of divine intervention in the life of the baby Jesus when his parents "went home by a different way" to escape danger at the hands of Herod.

And so it is today that we are gathered here to pray for discernment and guidance in terms of keeping these, our children, safe and well, that they might lead long and healthy lives in God's service. We pray that they may, in time, make the shift from summer fun to school-year discipline. We pray that they may learn not only academic subjects, but the courtesy of the heart. We live in a world where anger often leads to violence. Help these children learn alternatives to violence, we pray. School us all in how to see the viewpoints of others and stay the course in finding nonviolent solutions.

Protect them from participating in hurtful gossip about classmates, from participating in cruel schemes against each other. Teach them modes of cooperation. Allow them to come to know the importance of caring for their bodies and their spirits as well as their minds.

We pray also for the teachers present here. We are grateful for their willingness to guide our children. We pray for strength and stamina and discernment for them. May they know and honor their limitations as mere mortals, may they not be drawn into working so hard and so long that work becomes joyless, may they learn the fine art of self care of body, mind and spirit. May their classrooms be places of mutual respect and firm lovingkindness. May they never forget how important they are in the transmission of values, of culture, of learning. And may we never forget to express our gratitude to them.

God of Creation, your own dear son Jesus was a teacher. We know through reading Scripture every week that this was not an easy task. Grant these teachers wisdom and courage through his lineage and example. This we pray in Jesus' name, Amen.

"God of Grace and God of Glory" (v.1)

The New Century Hymnal

God of grace and God of glory,
on your people pour your power.
Crown your ancient church's story,
bring its bud to glorious flower.
Grant us wisdom, grant us courage,
for the facing of this hour.
For the facing of this hour.

Chapter 44

A Song of Trust

A message I once wrote begins with an explanation about why I wanted the children to be dismissed to Sunday School before the scriptures were read. The passages were gruesome but factual, that many Christians had been mocked, flogged, imprisoned, persecuted or killed for their faith (Hebrews 11). I wondered aloud what gave these people the courage to face an ugly end and not to flinch. I believe they knew something that we, too, are invited to know. They knew that we are not just bodies. They knew that we came from God and will return to God. They had been taught the love of Christ and had found the Christ in themselves. They were gifted with the peace that passes all understanding. Markers like time and location faded away. They were part of a grander scheme.

We are all invited to know this courage, faith, strength, resolve, determination and joy. We are invited to step away from the "values" of this world. Jesus gave us a choice. We can choose fear and spend the rest of our lives trying to control everybody else in the world so we can feel on top of things. Or, we can choose justice and mercy for all and find our spiritual strength and courage through finally recognizing who we are and where we fit in the Kingdom of God.

The first disciples left their families to follow Jesus. They experienced the strains of which Jesus spoke. While Jesus' words may upset us, they comforted those who were walking into the fire, so to speak. His words caused them to make sense of a world that opposed them and caused them to suffer. Perhaps they would also take with them these words from Jesus reported in the Gospel of John: "I have said this to you so that in me you may have peace. In the world you face persecution. But take courage: I have conquered the world!"

"Sermon Writer" publisher Dick Donovan, to whom this book is dedicated, shared a story about a minister named Dr. David Leininger, who preached a sermon in an election year entitled "Should the Church Stick its Nose into Things the Church Shouldn't Stick its Nose Into?" This pastor had received a nasty note from a congregation member and decided to name the sermon after her question. In response, his sermon outlined the work of Christians throughout history to take a stand in the public arena. He spoke of Peter taking a stand for the baptism of Gentiles. He spoke of Martin Luther taking a stand against the selling of indulgences by the Church of Rome. He spoke of William Wilberforce, who from the day of his adult baptism became an unrelenting foe of slavery in Britain. He told about Wilberforce basically giving his adult life for his Christian principles. He died three days after Parliament passed a law abolishing slavery for British citizens.

His work encouraged the opponents of slavery in the United States. People who agreed that slavery was evil did not give up. The United States had to go through its most terrible war—the Civil War—before it was able to put aside that unnecessary evil. It was a walk through fire—the fire of purification and the fire of judgment.

Many others would walk through fire during the civil rights movement, led by Martin Luther King Jr., whose hard teaching was that "those whom you would change, you must love first."

So how did Dr. Leininger end his sermon titled "Should the church stick its nose into things the church shouldn't stick its nose into"? He ended it this way. "THERE ARE NO SUCH THINGS! You see, the church says that Jesus Christ is Lord, and if he is not Lord OF all, he is not Lord AT all. Nothing in human life, not even politics and government, is outside the Lordship of Christ."

"MY FAITH, IT IS AN OAKEN STAFF" (v.1)
The New Century Hymnal

My faith, it is an oaken staff,
the traveler's well-loved aid;
My faith it is a song of trust,
sustains me undismayed.
I'll travel on and still be stirred
by silent thought or social word;
By all my perils undeterred,
a pilgrim unafraid.

Chapter 45

Spiritual Healing

Just what did the early Christians know that we may not know or yet believe? We wonder how they could endure captivity and gruesome deaths with love and courage. What gave these people the courage to face an ugly end and not flinch? They knew that we are not just bodies. They knew that we came from God and will return to God. They had been taught the love of Christ and had found the Christ in themselves. Markers like time and location faded away. They were part of a grander scheme, the whole tapestry of human history. They called this new consciousness "the kingdom of God." They were able to heal others and work miracles by holding onto their new identities in God.

In today's lesson, Jesus healed a woman by laying his hands upon her. To the early Christians, the laying on of hands was, for one thing, a part of the conversion experience. After believers were baptized in water, the outward declaration of inward faith, the believers had hands laid upon them. This was the sign of the reception of the Holy Spirit and of the oneness of God's people.

We well-educated and often highly literate folks are often very suspicious of receiving charisms, or the gifts of the Spirit. We're a lot more at home in our heads. The very thought of laying hands on someone seems strangely Pentecostal to us. And Pentecostal seems emotional and out of control. We don't like to let ourselves go there.

Many years ago I had a client who was an accountant for a large firm. He was a nominal Christian. He lived in daily fear that he could lose his job. He hated his job because it used not one iota of his creativity. But he loved the money and the security. He had a family to support. He seemed to be in danger of becoming what I call "dry wood," that is, those people who allow the life blood to drain out of them for reasons of safety, security, fear, or just lack of imagination.

We did some exploring of his creative side. He was delightfully verbal and skilled with the use of words. His days were "numbers," but his sessions were "words" and the exploration of possibilities. I don't know how it happened, but one Sunday night he decided to go to a Pentecostal church service in the town where he lived. He was stunned to discover that it touched him to the very core of his being.He was well educated, wore a suit to work every day and drove a nice car, but somehow none of that mattered in the presence of these folks and the power of the Holy Spirit.

Kathleen Norris, in her book *Amazing Grace: A Vocabulary of Faith*, tells of a doctoral student at Princeton who had a similar experience to that of my client. And Norris and her husband developed an unexpected friendship with an Assembly of God pastor.

After reflecting upon the seeming differences between Pentecostal worshippers (those who experience direct revelation) and the folks in her own mainline Protestant denomination, she had a kind of vision of all of them coming together, bearing each others' wounds, offering differing gifts. She envisioned a present Pentecost, where all could understand each other.

Perhaps you know someone who could receive a blessing from you, who could benefit greatly from your own belief that you can be a conduit for the Holy Spirit. All we have to do is get out of the Spirit's way and go where it leads us.

"Sweet, Sweet Spirit"
The New Century Hymnal

There's a sweet, sweet Spirit in this place,
and I know that it's the Spirit of the Lord;
there are sweet expressions on each face,
and I know they feel the presence of the Lord.
Sweet Holy Spirit, sweet heavenly Dove,
stay right here with us, filling us with your love;
And for these blessings, we lift our hearts in praise.
Without a doubt we'll know that we have been revived
when we shall leave this place.

Chapter 46
Conflict Resolution

I am grateful to Rev. Dick Donovan for his helpful research on today's Gospel lesson. And I am grateful to one of my Luther College religion teachers, Conrad Simonson, for writing a book called *In Search of God* that contains a beautiful illustration for this message. The message has to do with conflict resolution and reconciliation.

In his book, Simonson tells about a vacation with his parents and sister. They were at a cabin on a lake in northern Minnesota. It was a beautiful day. The sky was blue—just a few clouds to make it interesting. The lake was calm. It was perfect—the kind of day where tensions melt away and you just feel great.

But the family was **not** feeling great that day. Simonson's sister had returned from visiting their brother, who lived in Montana. When she began talking about that visit, it reminded their father that the brother had borrowed money but had failed to pay it back. The more the father thought about this, the angrier he got. Before long, the day was ruined.

Simonson responded by sitting down and writing a letter to his brother. He told his brother how his father's anger had spoiled the day—and how his mother hoped to see the absent brother—and how his father said, "Not until he does something about that loan."

The absent brother responded by writing his father a letter. He acknowledged his debt, laid out his financial situation, and explained why he could not pay off the loan at the moment. That was all it took. With that explanation, the father's anger evaporated. A few months later, the parents visited their son in Montana and all had a good time.

Then, about six months after that trip, the father and mother were involved in a serious automobile accident. The mother was grievously injured. Simonson called his brother, who came immediately to see his parents. Then the mother died. The father and the once-absent son—absent no longer—were together in their grief and able to comfort one another.

Simonson came to see that when he had initially written to the brother about the grievance, God had acted in his life to initiate that action. Before writing that letter, the conflict between father and absent son cast a pall on everything. But the letter pried the lid off the can of worms. It allowed the brother to see the mess and encouraged him to do something about it.

Fortunately, the brother responded. He wrote to his father and effected a reconciliation. Not everyone responds like that. The brother might have just let his father stew, but that would not have helped. Or he could have claimed poverty, or he could have told the father to go jump in a lake.

Instead, the brother, a decent man who was financially in over his head, did what he could. He explained his situation and asked for patience. That's all it took. And the father responded positively.

This story demonstrates how it is supposed to work among Christians when there is a problem. Conflict resolu-

tion begins with telling the truth in love, not grumbling behind people's backs, or being sarcastic, or passive-aggressive.
Donovan writes:

> Anyone who has been in the ministry for any length
> of time has seen it all. We have seen Christians angry
> at each other or at us. We have seen people get mad
> and quit the church. We have seen issues go round
> and round at board meetings. We have seen sus-
> picions and backbiting. We've heard gossip. We've
> seen it all and heard it all—and have been the target
> of a fair amount of it.
>
> So what should we do? Just sweep it under the rug
> and hope it will go away? That's what we often do.
> **But that wasn't Jesus' way.** Jesus always confronted
> conflict head-on—and that's what he wants us to do.

Donovan strongly emphasizes this point: Jesus wants us
to confront conflict head-on, **but he doesn't want us to win.**
Nor does he want us lose. He wants us to be reconciled to
our brother or sister. That's the real goal: reconciliation.

"DEAR GOD, EMBRACING HUMANKIND" (v. 1)
The New Century Hymnal

Dear God, embracing humankind,
forgive our foolish ways;
Reclothe us in our rightful mind,
in purer lives your service find,
in deeper reverence, praise.

Chapter 47

My Most-Loved Sermon, Part 1

My name is Guadalupe. I work in the kitchen at the Life Care Center in Evergreen, Colorado. The Life Care Center is a place that takes care of elderly and disabled people when their families can no longer care for them. Many of these people are brought into my dining room three times a day to eat the food I cook. Sometimes I catch their eye when they are enjoying my food. I feel a little bond with them, because I know that I will be old someday and I hope there will be someone to cook good food for me.

I grew up in a big city in Mexico. My father drove a truck for a grocery store chain. He made very little money. Once, when his truck had a flat tire, he paid to have it fixed himself because he was afraid he would be blamed for it and then let go from his work. There were twelve of us to feed, and he could not risk losing his job. My mother had to work also. She took in laundry from some of the wealthier people in the next neighborhood. She was never afraid of work. Sometimes I would wake up in the night and see her in the living room ironing clothes. She would hum to herself. We had no television for her to watch. I can still smell the steam that came from the iron when it touched the freshly laundered shirts.

On Sundays, we would dress nicely to prepare to go

to Mass. Mama would bake a special breakfast cake on Saturdays and we were never allowed to touch it until Sunday morning. It was sweet with honey and had nuts on top. Maybe that is why I am a cook today, because my mama made that cake with such love.

Our church was very special to me because it had a statue of Our Lady of Guadalupe. I loved to hear the stories about her appearances to my people through Juan Diego. She promised us that she would never leave us, she promised us that we would be all right. My Uncle Roberto told me that to him, she was like a warm lap he could crawl up onto whenever he felt tired or afraid. I loved her very deeply because she was mine. I had been named after her and she was mine.

Sometimes the priest would talk about the importance of keeping our faith in God even when we had tough times in our lives. Other times, he would talk about a great banquet hall where those of us who were poor would be invited to be the guests of honor. I wondered what this would be like. Would this mean I would live in a house like the ones who gave Mama their laundry lived in? Would it mean that my papa would not have to work so hard, or my mama iron into the night? I didn't understand these things, but I loved Jesus for saying them. I loved hearing him say that there was a kingdom where no one had to go without, and where things like big houses didn't matter. I loved Jesus' mother, too, and I knew in my heart that she had come to my people as Our Lady of Guadalupe.

Many years passed. One of my brothers began to sell

drugs under the influence of his gang. He was shot dead in broad daylight. We wept and wept but Mama and Papa had to keep working even with tears in their eyes. My little sister was hit by a car near our house. We could not afford the help she needed. Our Lady kept her alive, but she is crippled and cannot find work.

"How Lovely is Your Dwelling" (v.1)
The New Century Hymnal

How lovely is your dwelling,
O God, my hope and strength.
My spirit longs for shelter,
my flesh cries out for home,
Where even swallows nesting
beside your altar resting
Are ever praising you.

Chapter 48

My Most-Loved Sermon, Part 2

Imet Ramon, the man I would marry, at a street dance one night when I was seventeen. He wanted to be an auto mechanic and knew many things. He also had a brother in Denver and he longed to go to the United States. I was afraid. I loved my parents and my brothers and sisters and wanted to stay with them. But I also loved Ramon. We were married on June 17 in 1999. We went to the United States to visit Juan, Ramon's brother, and started the paperwork to become Americans.

Ramon and I were dreamers. We saw the television, we heard the radio. We thought everyone in America lived like movie stars or millionaires. We had stars in our eyes. It was very hard to find work here. It was just like home. There were drugs, there were gangs, there were mean bosses, there were hopeful priests. Why did we move here? I asked myself when our third child was born. What have we gained?

Sometimes I would crawl onto the lap of Our Lady at night and just cry and cry. She would comfort me somehow and dry my tears. I would think of Our Lord Jesus and how he wanted me to be the guest of honor at his wonderful table. I would take the Eucharist from the priest on Sundays and pray that there might be enough real food to feed my family. One day my friend Anita told me about a place in Evergreen that needed a cook. "I can cook!" I thought joyfully. I smelled again Mama's wonderful Sunday cake. "I will go with you to find out about cooking," I told Anita. And so it was that I came to work in the Life Care Center. My neighbor Gracia takes care of my children while I am at work. I like my job, but the hardest part is getting there. There were 205 inches of snow in Evergreen last year. It is a very steep highway to get there from my house. Many times my old car could not make the trip, even though Ramon keeps it in very good condition. Sometimes I wish we could live in Evergreen. I would not have to miss so much work that way. It makes me very nervous to drive in so much snow. Sometimes I can't get home at night. It is very hard to work in Evergreen and live in Denver.

I am afraid to live in Evergreen, just like I was afraid to live in America. I know my neighbors here in Denver, and even if our neighborhood is dangerous, it is mine. Would people in Evergreen accept me and my family if we lived there? Would there be any priests who could help us find housing for the little money we make? I heard a man in the hallway at the Life Care Center talking about how expensive it is to live in Evergreen. Even people with pretty good pay-checks can't afford to live there.

I know that Our Lady will find a way for me. She has watched over my people for many years. I believe that she will find some hearts and some hands in Evergreen and plant the vision in their minds of God's banquet table. I see it my mind sometimes. I will bring my mother's Sunday cake, and someone else will bring wildflowers from a meadow. A man will bring some elk meat that he is proud of. We will all laugh together and tell of the foods of our childhood. No one will feel poor, and everyone will feel rich. Isn't this what our Lord saw for us? I know Our Lady is at work for me. She stays up long into the night planting seeds of love in people's hearts while they sleep. I hope you will come to the banquet with me to taste my cake. And I cannot wait to see what you bring.

Author's note: I wrote this message perhaps in or near the year 2008. Many people approached me after worship to ask how they could help this woman. I had to confess that she was entirely fictional, and that she represented my fervent hope for affordable workforce housing in Evergreen. I am so delighted to tell you that on October 12, 2018 there was a groundbreaking ceremony here for 54 units of affordable workforce housing. The organization I helped to found, AT HOME in Evergreen, Inc., was well represented.

"How Lovely Is Your Dwelling" (v.2)
The New Century Hymnal

How blessed are those whose travels
are strengthened by your hand,
who pass through shadowed valleys
and find refreshing springs.
Your rain falls soft as kindness
 on all your faithful pilgrims
until they come to you.

Chapter 49

Prayers for Artists

I have waited for this Sunday for some time now. It is the very first Sunday of what I call "Second Sunday Singers," although it will include musicians and dancers of all sorts as it grows and develops. Once, when writing a grant application, I dreamed up a program called "Society for the Appreciation of Imperfect Musicians." In my mind, I saw Joya continuing to bring forth wonderful music as she did last January in this sanctuary, when five women sang "Steal Away" a capella, meaning without accompaniment. They did this with just one hour of practice. To my way of thinking, the Holy Spirit accompanied them. Refreshing, renewing, making all things possible.

Today, in this room, we have heard the fruit of such an endeavor once more. And today's lesson from the book of James instructs us as to how we may receive our artists so that we may be people of faith and NOT judges of imperfect artists. Perhaps if you were once a person whose creativity was harshly judged, you now house that judge in your own being. The job of those of us who become "the audience" is to silence that judge and become encouragers of art.

I have taken a bold leap today and have rewritten parts of our lesson from James to apply not to the rich and poor in financial terms, but the rich and the poor in terms of who has "arrived" as an artist, and who has not. Here is what I came up with:

My brothers and sisters, do you with your acts of favoritism really believe in our glorious Lord Jesus Christ? For if a person with numerous recording contracts, famous throughout the land for singing, comes into your assembly, and if a person whom you have never heard sing a note also comes in, and if you take notice of the one who is famous and say, "Have a seat here, please," while to the one who is unknown you say, "Stand there," or "Sit at my feet," have you not made distinctions among yourselves, and become judges with evil thoughts? Listen, my beloved brothers and sisters. Has not God chosen the unproven in the world to be provers of faith and to be heirs of the kingdom that God has promised to those who love God?

A guide that has helped a number of people I know is called *The Artist's Way: A Spiritual Path to Higher Creativity*, by Julia Cameron. This text is a field guide for those wading through the swamps of self-deprecation to arrive at a place of healthy creativity. Using some of Cameron's principles, I'd like to share some stories with you about recovering the creative potential with which *you* were born.

I once had an artist as a client in psychotherapy. She wasn't in therapy because of her art. She was in therapy because of a very troubled marriage. But it is the artist part of this woman I'd like to talk about today. One of the first things we had to do was deconstruct her notion of who God is. She had a toxic old idea that God's will for her and her will for herself were at opposite ends of the table. So, if she wanted to be an artist, God would make sure she became a drudge instead. The author Cameron dealt with this dilemma herself. While writing about the god she did believe in and the God she would like to believe in, she was struck with this thought, "What if God is a woman and she is on my side?" She warns her readers, "If you are still dealing with a god consciousness that has remained unexamined since childhood, you are probably dealing with a toxic god." She asks, "What would a nontoxic God think of your creative goals? Might such a God really exist?"

A man named Nachmanovitch wrote a book about improvisation. In it, he writes:

> At the age of four, a child I knew drew extraordinary vibrant, imaginative trees. Crayon, chalk, colored pens, and silly putty were all useful. These trees were remarkable in how clearly they showed the bulbous lobes and branchy veins of individual leaves in a kind of cubist, all-the-way-around view that would have delighted Picasso. Meticulous observation of real trees, and a certain daring that is characteristic of four-year-olds, combined to produce those striking artworks.

> By the age of six, this child had gone through a year of first grade and had begun drawing lollipop trees just like the other kids. Lollipop trees consist of a single blob of green, representing the general mass of leaves with details obliterated, stuck up on top of a

brown stick, representing a tree trunk. Not the sort of place real frogs would live.

When we encounter a stifling of our creative genius at an early age, it may be a very long time until we allow that creative but deeply wounded child to raise his or her voice again. You see, we have stuffed that painful chapter in our lives away into a cellar called "the unconscious," wherein hurt instead of freedom has come to dictate our lives. However, in Cameron's words, "Fulfilling our creativity is a sacred trust." May we all find that now.

"Sing Praise to God, Our Highest Good" (v.2)
The New Century Hymnal

Creation thanks you, Holy One:
You made us and renew us.
Delighted at what You have done,
You show Your greatness through us.
So may all living things proclaim the
wonder of their Maker's name:
to God give praise and glory.

Chapter 50

When Love Bursts Forth

Midway through my seminary education, I was required to read a book entitled *Paul: Apostle of the Heart Set Free*, by F.F. Bruce. It had a deep impact upon me. I, like most people, have an internal "judge" who can get quite vocal when she perceives that I or another person have erred. She has been known to go on the warpath with people whom she feels are out of line. And of course, she has thrashed me at regular intervals.

Paul, before his conversion, was such a person. He was a strong Jewish man of good upbringing and Roman citizenship. It is widely held that he was a persecutor of Christians. His inner judge was quite activated against Christians, whom he viewed as a threat to Judaism. We all know the story of how he was met on the road to Damascus by the risen Christ. That he was bathed in brilliant light that blinded him. And that when he recovered from this incident, and processed it, and experienced himself as a new man, he was filled with love and energy to preach the good news of free grace, which we call the gospel. Love burst forth in Paul.

Here are a few lines from F.F. Bruce:

> Love is a more potent incentive in doing the will of God that legal regulations and fear of judgment could ever be. (p. 19)

> The written code kills, because it declares the will of God without imparting the power to do it, and pro-

nounces the death sentence on those who break it.
The Spirit gives life and with the life he imparts the
inward power as well as the desire to do the will of
God. (p. 200)

Bruce helped me to understand what he believes are
Paul's four most important teachings: (1) True religion is
not a matter of rules and regulations. (2) In Christ men and
women have come of age and are to live as responsible sons
and daughters of God. (3) People matter more than things,
more than principles, more than causes, and (4) Unfair discrimination on the grounds of race, religion, class or sex is
an offense against God and humanity alike.

In my life as a psychotherapist, I worked with many people who suffered with depression and who truly questioned
whether they wished to go on living. In his later years, Paul
was a person who weighed the assets and liabilities of remaining alive. In verses 22-26 of chapter 1 in Philippians, he
is "hard pressed" to choose between life in the flesh and life
with Christ. He elects to continue his ministry for the sake
of those who still needed to be encouraged in their faith.

I once read a story about Albert Wallace, a Vietnam vet-
eran who drifted for decades after the war, mostly between
Widefield and Colorado Springs. His only companions were
a half gallon jug of cheap wine and a Colt 5. He spent at least
14 years homeless in Colorado. He drifted from shelter to
shelter. In 1991 he took refuge in a Red Cross shelter and it
was there that he experienced an epiphany. We are not told
the details of this event. Perhaps it was something like Paul's
experience on the road to Damascus. At any rate, it took
Wallace several years to rebuild his life, but he did so, with

the help of the Veterans Administration. He had promised himself early on that he would do something for that shelter that had taken him in back in 1991, and on the day before Mother's Day in 1993, he decided to fulfill his old pledge. Initially he wanted to buy a television set for the shelter, but to his own surprise, he bought dozens of roses. He took them to the shelter on Mother's Day and handed them out to the women there. Their tearful gratitude prompted him to bring dinner for them, too. He said, "And then it came to me. Why don't I just do it for everybody?" This began a ministry that would last until his death in 2005, a ministry of providing for the needy through weekly chicken dinners.

He took over the Good News Foundation, which serves low-income and homeless people in southern Colorado. He calculated that since 1994, the foundation provided 90,000 Thanksgiving meals, 30,000 Christmas suppers and 1,000 pairs of eyeglasses. They sent 500 needy children to summer camp in Divide. He would tell his co-workers, "Working for the Lord does not pay much, but the retirement is out of this world." Love broke forth in the life of Albert Wallace. It can break forth in all of us when we surrender our lives and wills to God. We can reclaim our souls and our moral compasses. We can find a reason to go on living.

"Won't You Let Me Be Your Servant" (v. 1)
The New Century Hymnal

Won't you let me be your servant,
let me be as Christ to you?
Pray that I may have the grace
to let you be my servant, too.

Chapter 51

Faith, Dogs and Mustard Seeds

In the middle of her life, my grandmother encountered a weekend from hell. She and my grandfather and their three daughters made that heavy-hearted trip to another town to bury my grandma's mother. Perhaps some present recall a sad trip to bury a mother. I know I do. Somehow the concept of "home" felt more precious after her passing. But my grandmother, upon burying her mother, did not return to an increased sense of home and security, but to another soul-wrenching crisis. For some reason, my grandparents had allowed their only son to stay home from the burial. It seems he and a friend were horsing around in my grandfather's study. My grandpa was a railway postal clerk and was required to wear a gun. He kept it in his desk. My grandparent's only son was killed accidentally by a friend.

I tend to think that if these events had happened to me, I might be sorely tempted to abandon my faith. My grandparents were people of very strong faith. They might have said, "Hey, God, we've been your people. We've tithed, we've served others, we pray, we read scripture. How could you do this to us?" They might have been like the disciples in Luke 17, looking for an easy recipe to follow. But Jesus warned against this type of attitude which has to do more with earning rewards than with faith. Jesus modeled a kind of servant-ministry and he calls us to it.

In the words of Dick Donovan, "He came to earth, not

in Rome, but in Palestine—not with a silver spoon in his mouth—not to sit on a throne, but to hang on a cross. If we have a quarrel with the demands of discipleship, we must address our objections to the one who had modeled the kind of sacrifice that he asks us to make."

My grandma always wore a little glass globe on her watch band that contained a mustard seed. It is possible that during her weekend from hell, her faith could have shrunk to that size. But it never disappeared. She remained faithful in service, in prayer and in scripture reading all the days of her life. She was my spiritual mentor.

Perhaps if mustard seeds do not speak to you, a story about a dog might. You may be aware that Native Americans believe that animals carry certain medicine for our spirits. Just as Communion is *food* for our spirits, animals can be *medicine* for our spirits. The medicine that dogs carry is Loyalty. The dog has been considered the servant of humanity throughout history. Dogs offer friendship and protection. They are able to transcend bad treatment by their owners, not out of stupidity, but from a deep and compassionate understanding of human shortcomings. Dogs have much to teach us about loyalty and faith. They don't just love us when we feed them. Their loyalty runs deeper than mere obedience, as Jesus wants ours to do.

We once had a dog named George that we raised alongside our children. As he grew older, he became blind and epileptic. He could no longer do tricks or fetch. He loved being outdoors and we walked him with care. We came to see that he was ultimately showing us that **loving and being loved** is what life is about. Performance is not part of the package.

We, like the disciples, ask God to increase our faith. Sometimes the seeds of faith will lie dormant in us. This is part of life. But we must believe that they will bloom again. And like our friend the dog, we must stay faithful to the One who will help these seeds to flourish. Faith is not just about thanking God for the blossoms, but also thanking God for abiding with us during times of pain and dormancy.

"BE THOU MY VISION" (v.1)
The Chalice Hymnal

Be thou my vision, O Lord of my heart:
naught be all else to me, save that thou art.
Thou my best thought by day or by night,
waking or sleeping, thy presence my light.

Chapter 52

Releasing Old Scripts

This is the final chapter of this book, and I hope that in some ways it has helped readers to launch new beginnings, based on faith. I have derived much pleasure from putting these words together. Now, it is time to find a publisher, and I am determined to listen for the Spirit's nudgings for the next step.

In 2008, I heard a woman speaker tell a wonderful story about her life and her faith. Because of the financial crisis in that year, she elected to speak about "the fear of financial insecurity."

She took us back to the early days of her marriage and family life. Her husband had been a building contractor. Often, builders will build a house on "speculation" and hope that someone will buy it. The builder will sometimes move into that house until it sells. However, for whatever reasons, the house did not sell.

The woman and her husband were somewhat new to the Christian Science faith, but they knew that fear was an invention of the mind, and that their prayers would settle them back into their identity in God. The bank foreclosed on the house and the couple, with their young children, went to live in the garage of friends. Is this something you would be comfortable doing? Well, faith motivated them to keep a good attitude and the children did not even realize that anything was "wrong."

The wife went to a nearby city to try to find work through a temporary work agency. I believe she was trained as a teacher, but no positions were available. After a particularly frustrating day with temp agencies, the wife went home discouraged. Her husband approached her. He asked her, "If you could do anything in the world, what would you like to do?" She paused for a moment, and to their surprise she answered that she would like to be an interior decorator. The husband asked her where she would work. She responded that she had come through a small town that very afternoon and had seen a furniture store with carpet sales. Her husband asked her to find child care and off they went.

The owner of the shop was surprised to hear of the woman's plan, for he was about to begin a search for a decorator. It was mid-afternoon, and he showed the woman a blueprint of the house that a customer wished to decorate. He told her that she had one hour to make a plan and produce a cost analysis. She had never done such a thing, but she commenced to work and completed a plan. The shop owner was impressed and hired her on the spot. She went on to earn three times more than she would have as a teacher.

In her book, *Love Without End: Jesus Speaks*, Glenda Green speaks of how, through machinations of our minds, we create a script. Our minds prefer structured reality. Our minds want to pre-guess and predetermine what life is about. The script we create can become a great trap. And few of us are able to move beyond that script.

Some Pharisees hoped to set a trap for Jesus by asking him if people of faith needed to pay taxes. Certainly, since time immemorial, people have believed in the script that says, "I can't be happy until I have financial security" and paying taxes seems to some like a roadblock to financial wealth. But Jesus wanted to move people out of the world of structure and into life in the Spirit, which is mediated by the heart, not the mind. He encouraged people to abandon their need for financial security and relax and just "be."

Scripture tells us that the love of money is the root of all evil. The love of money comes from fear, for we believe that money can solve our problems. Green tells us that greed is an obsessive desire which attempts to nourish and supply the needs of life, but without love.

A man once told me that brain scientists have concluded that there is only a two percent likelihood that a person can escape their life script and begin to formulate new responses to old problems. Jesus continually taught people how to change our minds and free our hearts. The old script is to work a problem to death with our minds. The new way is to open our hearts and minds to new responses... just like the woman speaker did. An interior designer? Who would have thought? "I don't need to know the design my life will take, I only need to trust the Designer." Amen.

A SONG I ONCE HEARD:
I love you, Lord. You heard my cry
and pitied every groan.
Long as I live, and troubles rise,
I'll hasten to thy throne.

About the Author

Ann Bolson's career evolved from nursing to education to counseling and to ministry. Her Doctor of Ministry degree was earned in 2000 from The Chicago Theological Seminary. Her project in ministry was entitled "Searching for the God of Grace: Psychotherapy and Spiritual Accompaniment with Wounded Christians."

Ann and her husband Steve reside in the foothills of the Rocky Mountains where they enjoy daily visits from deer, elk and wild birds. They are the parents of two children and the grandparents of two boys and two grand-dogs.

Ann has been a member of "Mountain Writers" for over a ten years. She enjoys hiking, yoga, swimming, baking, playing her flute and having coffee with friends.